What Others Are Saying
Hollywood

"I have known Chambers Stevens for almost twenty years and it doesn't surprise me in the least that his ability to zoom in on bull's eye monologues for today's youth is accurate and tasteful. As a theatre arts veteran secondary teacher of three decades, I can shout from the rooftops how frustrating it is to match monologue, young actor, and interest level in a happy and comfortable marriage of talent. I have spent countless hours at Drama Bookshop on Times Square searching for appropriate monologue and audition material. Finally, the search is over!"

—KENT CATHCART, DRAMA & SPEECH TEACHER
MCGAVOCK HIGH SCHOOL, NASHVILLE, TN

"Like the other entries in this series, this volume {Sensational Scenes For Teens} offers young actors fresh audition material written by an acting coach who works with kids...The contemporary urban and suburban settings coupled with culturally neutral names allow for racial and ethnic diversity. Libraries that serve growing drama programs would certainly want to consider purchasing this title."

—SCHOOL LIBRARY JOURNAL

"Stevens is one of the most respected acting coaches in Hollywood."

—THE PITTSBURG TRIBUNE-REVIEW

VIRGINIA BEACH, VA

"Chambers really connects with teenagers. He's written monologues that are the essence of teenagers. He's written about our fears and joys, our lives. It was a privilege to study with him. He really knows what he is writing about."

—JENNIE HILL, STUDENT ACTRESS
NITRO HIGH SCHOOL

"My friends almost tore the *Magnificent Monologues* up deciding who was going to read it next."

—STEPHANIE LANE, STUDENT ACTOR, MT. JULIET JUNIOR HIGH

Magnificent Monologues for Teens

What Others Are Saying About the Hollywood 101 series

"What energy! What enthusiasm! What a great afternoon! Chambers and his team put on a top-notch event for kids, customers and booksellers alike. A big success. Top rate all the way."
—JOHN SCHATZEL, *COMMUNITY RELATIONS MANAGER*
BARNES & NOBLE, SANTA MONICA, CA

"In my thirty years of working in professional and community theatre, I find Mr. Stevens' work to be an exuberant breath of fresh air."
—JOHN MARSHALL *MUSICAL DIRECTOR*
CHARLESTON LIGHT OPERA GUILD

"Your son is funnier than the kids you see on TV. Your daughter has begged to be an actress since she was 3. But how can you help them break into show business? LA-based children's acting coach Chambers Stevens can answer that question!"
—AMY WHITE, STAFF WRITER
THE BAKERSFIELD CALIFORNIAN

"Working with Chambers and his material, I scored my first part in a movie! It was a blast. I've never had so much fun."
—REID GODSHAW, ACTOR
VAN WILDER PARTY LIAISON
NATIONAL LAMPOON

"Chambers is articulate, interesting, engaging and very knowledgeable about the biz. He was among my top ten favorite guests. A real pro!"
—ANDREA SHEA KING, HOST "WHAT'S SHAKING!"
WMMB AM 1240 TALK RADIO, MELBOURNE FL

The Teens' Monologue Source for Every Occasion!

Hollywood 101

MAGNIFICENT MONOLOGUES for teens

"The Teens' Monologue Source for Every Occasion!"

by

Chambers Stevens

SANDCASTLE PUBLISHING LLC

ChildrenActingBooks.com

South Pasadena, California USA
www.ChildrenActingBooks.com

Magnificent Monologues for Teens: The Teens' Monologue Source for Every Occasion!

Sandcastle Publishing LLC
Post Office Box 3070
South Pasadena, CA 91031-6070
Phone/Website (323) 255-3616, www.ChildrenActingBooks.com

Publisher's Cataloging in Publication
(Provided by Quality Books, Inc.)

Stevens, Chambers.
    Magnificent monologues for teens : the teens'
monologue source for every occasion! / Chambers
Stevens. -- 1st ed.
    p. cm. -- (Hollywood 101 ; 4)
    Includes bibliographical references and index.
    ISBN: 1-883995-11-6

    1. Monologues--Juvenile literature. 2. Acting--
Juvenile literature. 3. Teenagers--Drama--Juvenile
literature. 4. Acting--Auditions [1. Monologues. 2. Acting.]
I. Title. II. Series.

PN2080.S74 2002   792'.02
                           QBI02-701444

First Printing 5/02

Printed and bound in America
16 15 14 13   12 11 10 9th

Table of Contents

Dedication

TO

PEARL

THE GREATEST STORYTELLER I'VE EVER KNOWN.

MAY HER WORDS LIVE FOREVER IN MY HEART.

Welcome to Hollywood 101 and the wonderful, exciting, magnificent world of monologues.

For the last 15 years, I have been a kids/teen acting coach. Just as football, basketball, and baseball players, have a coach, most actors do too. I have coached kids in shows for WB, Nickelodeon, Disney, CBS, NBC, ABC, and FOX, plus countless movies, commercials and theater productions. I have helped kids get agents, managers, Broadway shows—even the lead in their school play! And in all that time, my biggest challenge has been finding great monologues for teenagers.

Did you notice I said, *"great?"* That's because to get a part in a play, movie or even a commercial, "good" is not enough. Always strive for magnificent! I call monologues "The Olympics of acting". Why? Because when the director says "action", it's just you, on the stage, showing your stuff. For many actors this is a scary experience. So, when you go on stage, you want to have the best material/script possible, right?! That's what you'll find in this book.

The problem I've found with other monologue books is, well, the monologues don't sound like teenagers talking! They use words and "slang" that I've never heard except in fifties television shows. In **Magnificent Monologues for Teens** there are 52 monologues all 100% tested by some of the best young actors I know!

They cover a range of subjects, emotions and actions. And best of all, they are fun to perform. Why is that so important? Ask yourself. If acting isn't fun, why are you doing it?

QUESTION: What is a monologue and why do I need one?

Good question. I'm glad you asked. The short answer is: A monologue is one person talking (unlike a "scene" which is two or more people talking).

Even Shakespeare used monologues in his plays. His best known one is in *Romeo and Juliet*, when Juliet, standing on her balcony after the party where she first met Romeo, asks, "Romeo, Romeo, wherefore art thou, Romeo?" Almost everyone has heard of that line. And how about *Hamlet's* "To be or not to be." That's also a monologue.

Okay, fine, you say. I now know what a monologue is. But why do I need one?

Two reasons, really: First, if you are an actor or actress, which I assume you are, then I'm sure one of your goals is to . . . act! In anything you can: plays, television, film, commercials. Now, the only way you are going to be able to do this is by AUDITIONING. (Notice I didn't say try outs. Try outs are for sport team). An actor or actress auditions for directors and producers who make theatre, TV, and films by showing them how he/she acts.

What better way to show them your stuff than to do a Magnificent Monologue. You get it?

Monologues are the easiest dramatic work to audition with. They're short. Audition pieces, (another way to describe monologues), should never be longer than three minutes. I've coached many teen actors who have won jobs just by performing a great monologue.

The second reason you need great monologues as an actor/actress is also very important. Working on monologues has to be fun! If it's not, it will show in your performance.

In this book, you will meet some of the strangest, smartest, wackiest teenagers I know. Some of them are cruel or sad. Some of them are heroic. And I bet some of them are going through the same problems and challenges you are going through in your life. But most of all, they are all fun to pretend to be.

And if acting isn't fun, then why are you doing it?

Magnificent Comedic Monologues!

The Teens' Monologue Source for Every Occasion!

Ashley
(How to Attract Boys)

Note: Create a very strange laugh. This will make the monologue funnier.

(Ashley talks to her friend, Leah)

Leah! If I have to hear one more time how many guys like you, I am going to throw up. That's all you talk about.
(She imitates Leah.)
"Bobby was flirting with me after history. Oh, and I got a note from Travis. He likes my eyes. And did I tell you Steven is massively in love with me?" Yes, you have! About a million times!!! How do you think that makes me feel? Guys never ask me out. Never!!! I don't understand it. I'm better looking than you. Oh, don't look at me that way. You know it's true. And, I'm <u>nicer</u> than you, too. I don't understand it. What's your secret? Wait! Don't tell me. It's probably something stupid, like, you always laugh at their jokes or something.
(A beat.)
That's it?!! That's how you get them to like you? I can't believe it's that simple. What, you just pretend to laugh?
Wait! <u>That</u> is what you do. This morning in homeroom you were talking to Christian, and you were laughing your little hinny off. And I've heard Christian's jokes. They ain't that funny. I can do this. This is easy. I'll just walk up to the first good-looking boy I see and go—
(She does this HUGE fake laugh.)
Wait. That might scare him. I better start small.
(Ashley does this really small silly laugh.)
No. That sounds stupid. Maybe I should mix the two.
(She starts off with this huge laugh and then suddenly drops to this small little laugh.)
No. That makes me sound like they should cart me off to the loony bin. This is harder than it looks. Who knew flirting was so complicated?

Brittany
(The Fashion Police)

(Brittany comes running in, blowing her whistle.)

Hold it! Yeah you with the orange jacket! Stop!
(Brittany walks up to the fashion victim.)
I've already warned you once this week, so I'm sorry, but I'm going to have to give you a ticket. I mean come on girl. An orange jacket and a purple top? Where did you learn fashion? And those socks. They don't even match...each other. One is canary yellow and the other one is more sunflower. Come on, this is not the circus.

Speaking of clowns, you're wearing way way too much make-up. What do you put it on with, a paint brush? You must have a whole tube of lipstick on those lips. Make up is supposed to enhance your beauty, not obliterate it. And your mascara is way too heavy. You look like you were running without a sports bra and you gave yourself two black eyes.

Speaking of bras not only is your strap showing but so is the hair under your arms which you FORGOT TO SHAVE! This is not the sixties! Buy yourself a razor.
(She writes out the ticket.)
You have so many infractions I can't fit them all on one ticket. I'm going to have to take you in. Maybe this time you'll learn what good taste is. Next time you decide to leave the house, remember, the fashion police are watching you.

Billie
(Trailer Park Dreams)

(Billie is sitting on the couch. She yells towards the other room.)

Shut up in there before I tell your Mama!
(To audience)
Kids. I hate them!
Which is a sad thang when you're a babysitter.
(Yelling towards the other room)
Shut up! I'm talkin' in here.
(To audience)
Little Jimmy's P.O.'d 'cause Bubba's ridin' his Big Wheel.
(She yells towards the other room again.)
If you two don't be quiet, I'm gonna snatch you bald headed.
(To audience)
That did it. They know I'm mean enough to be serious.

See, I'm the babysitter for everyone in the trailer park. All the mama's dump their youngin's off, and then go and play cards. Then, who ever wins, has to pay me. Pretty good deal ain't it?

Last week I made 7 dollars. Bought me some perfume at the drug store. Obsession. I like to mix it with my Dad's Old Spice and make my own perfume. I call it Billie's Breath. That's my name—Billie. Someday, in trailer parks all across the country, people will be wearin' my perfume. And I'll be rich and give all my money to my Mama, so she can leave my step-dad, Ray.

(cont. next page)

Billie
(Trailer Park Dreams cont.)

He's a no-good. Actually, he's worse, but Mama doesn't like me cussin'. And her and I will move up to Atlanta. And get us a car. And if Ray tries to find us, we'll drive away.

Ain't cars wonderful thangs? They take you anywhere you want to go. That's why Mama doesn't have one. Because Ray knows if she has a car, she is outta here. When I was little, I used to dream that my Big Wheel was big enough to take me and Mama away. But that's just dreamin'. Gettin' rich off my own perfume is a much better idea.

Caroline
(Sing Your Problems Away)

Note: Even though Caroline's songs are silly, she takes them very seriously.

(Caroline walks on stage with her guitar.)

Hello. My name is Caroline Kryenski.
And I guess you can tell from my guitar that I'm a singer. Sorry if I'm a little nervous, but this is my first open mike. My first song is about my dog, Fluffy, who was recently run over by a car. It's called "Fluffy Watch Out!"

(She sits down, strums a few chords, and starts to sing.)
"Fluffy.
You're so cute running in the street.
Oh, no! A car!
Now Fluffy is flat!
Fluffy!
You're splattered on the street!
Looks like I'm going to have to get a cat.
Fluffy.
Watch out!"

(Applause) Thank you. Music has always been my dream. Actually I had a great dream last night. My head was this pumpkin and I kept spitting out the seeds. But that's another story. My next song is dedicated to my ex-boyfriend, Zack, otherwise known as the jerk who dumped me.

(cont. next page)

Caroline
(Sing Your Problems Away cont.)

(Singing)

"Zack.
You're a jerk.
A big jerk
A huge jerk.
A massive jerk.
Zack. Zack. Zack.
Jerk. Jerk. Jerk."

(She plays a big chord. And then stands up to take a bow.)
You are too kind. Okay. My next song isn't really a song. It's more of a dance. It's called: "Fluffy comes back from the dead and beats up Zack."

(Caroline lies on the floor. She jumps up like a dog. Then she runs to the other side of the stage and plays Zack lifting weights. Then she turns into Fluffy again. Slowly Fluffy sneaks up on Zack. Caroline runs back and forth on the stage doing a wild dance playing both Fluffy and Zack. It ends with a wild fight scene. Caroline is both victim and bully. When it is over she takes a grand bow.)

Thank you, Thank you. Well, my time is up. I'll be here next week when I'm going to be performing my new song, "Peanut Butter is a great face cream." Thank you.

Carrie
(The Confession)

(Carrie is trying to sneak in to her house, when her parents turn on the light.)

Oh! Mom! Dad! You scared me!
(She laughs.)
You're probably wondering why I'm just now getting home. Well...I ran out of gas. Well, I didn't run out...Marc did. It was an accident. You know his Dad's car is a real gas-guzzler. And we were stuck on the side of the road...well, not on the side of the road. We were more like parked...on Lover's Leap. I'm not really sure how we got there. I think it was when Marc ran that red light and the cops started chasing us. Yeah, that was it! And we out ran them, Dad! *(She whoops.)* You would be proud. Marc is a good driver. Those cops never had a chance.

So, anyway, we ended up on Lover's Leap. We were talking and...stuff. Well, mainly stuff. Mom, let me tell you, Marc is one heck of a kisser. And so, after a couple of hours of this, he decided to take me home. And whoops. We were out of gas. So, we had to walk down the hill, and we flagged down a cop. And guess what? It was the same one that was chasing us earlier. So he took Marc to jail. His parents had to ball him out. And Marc's dad is sooo nice. He gave me a ride home.

So, I hope that clears it up. See you tomorrow. *(She turns away, then turns back.)* Oh, yeah, before I forget, Marc and I are going to the movies on Saturday. That is if he's not in prison. Good night.

Danielle
(I've Got A Dork For A Dad)

(Danielle walks up to her Dad).

Dad, we need to talk.
Dad, listen up!
Stop reading! This is important.
Okay, I'm just going to say it.
Dad, you're a dork.
What? You are! Look at your hair. You don't have any. Your
head is way too shiny. And that moustache has got to go. Look
at it. You can tell you had corn flakes for breakfast. And that
suit. Dad, please, it is so disco. Last time you washed it, it
shrunk. And you look like someone stuffed you in it.
How are you ever going to find me another Mom when you
look so strange?
What? You have a date tonight?
Go, Dad, Go! Okay, look, it's too late to fix you up. But at least
brush your teeth. It smells like something died inside your
mouth.

Gina
(The Being-Dumped Blues)

(Gina is fighting with her boyfriend.)

So, wait, let me get this straight!

You're dumping me?

Me?

Hello!

What do you think you are? So fine?

No! I'll tell you what you are! You are dirt!

And you are not dumping me. Got that?

I am dumping you.

As of this moment, consider yourself dumped!

And don't be coming to me when you're fat and ugly, and you turn on the television, and you see me looking all good.

Because I'm not taking your fat, ugly, butt back. No way. So, why don't you just get out of here?

As of this moment, I am officially single!

And I don't want you hanging around me giving people the wrong idea that I care about you.

Where are you going?

Please, don't leave me.

I love you!

Pleeeeeeeeeese!!!!

Kiki

(For The Love Of Pete?)

(Kiki is yelling at her friend, Chrissy.)

You think I'm a genius? You're damn right. I AM a genius, but I'm still not giving you my math homework.
Give it up, Chrissy. Do it yourself sometimes.
Oh, please! Don't even go there.
The teachers may believe that phony "But I've been sick" stuff.
No, I'm not giving it to you.
I worked for an hour on this and...
What?
No way. No way.
You have a note that Pete Arbukle wrote to Jimmy Barnes saying how much he likes me? Oh, my gosh. OH MY GOSH!
Give it to me.
What?
For my homework?
This is not fair! I worked...
(Chrissy starts to walk off.)
Don't go! I'll trade.
(Kiki gives her homework to Chrissy. And gets the letter in return.)
Oh, my gosh. I can't believe this. I knew he liked me!
I knew it! I knew it!
Wait! This isn't Pete's handwriting.
He doesn't dot his "I's" with little hearts.
Wait a minute, you wrote this.....Chrissy?
(Looks up and Chrissy's gone.)
CHRISSY!!!!!!
(Kiki stomps away.)

Lara
(Spazmanian Devil)

(Lara is very hyper.)

Everybody says I'm such a spaz, which is totally not true, 'cause if I were a spaz, I would be spazzy, which is totally different from what I am.

Yesterday, Gary walked up to me at work, and he's all like, "calm down" and I'm like "what?" and he's like "calm down" and I'm like, "whatever", and he says I am such a spaz. Which is really ironic 'cause Gary is so hyper, and he's saying I'm a spaz?

So, the manager sees us talking, and she's like, "calm down" and Gary says, "that's what I've been telling her", and she's like, "both of you calm down", and Gary is like "what?", and she says, "Gary, you are such a spaz." And I start laughing like, *(She laughs really hard.)*, 'cause its really funny, and I'm laughing so loud that people can hear me all over the store, and the manager is like, "calm down" and Gary is, like, laughing, too, 'cause I sound really stupid. And the more we laugh, the madder the manager gets, and then I'm laughing so hard I can't breathe, so, I start jumping up and down to, you know, get some oxygen in my lungs, and I guess I looked really dumb 'cause Gary starts laughing more, and then he can't breathe either, so, he starts jumping up and down, and all the customers are looking at us. And the manger is yelling, "Lara, Gary stop that!" But we can't hear her 'cause we're jumping up and down, and then Gary trips and falls over these CDs and they go flying everywhere. And one of them lands on the floor under my foot, and I fall down, and as I'm falling, my arms swing out like this, and I knock down the manager, and she goes flying over this display of candles, and they smash all over the floor. So, Gary and I stop, and we're looking at her, and she is not happy, and she's like, "you guys are so fired", and we're like, "why?", and she's like, "'cause you guys are, like, Spazes", which is totally not true.

Why does everybody misunderstand me?

Leah
(The Talk-A-Holic)

(Leah is dialing her phone.)

(On the phone) Brittany? Oh, hi, Mrs. Plitt. Can I speak to Brittany? Okay, well, please tell her that I called. Thank you.
(Leah hangs up and dials another number.)
I hate these things. Ashley, it's me. Call me. I'm at home. I might go out later, so, I'll take my cell. If my battery goes dead or something, and I don't return your call, then beep me. You have all my numbers, but call me at home first. See ya. Oh, and wait 'til I tell you what Sam asked me at lunch! Call to find out.
(She hangs up and dials another number.)
Hey, Caleb, can I speak to Ruth? I don't know the password. Look, don't be a jerk. Let me...that's a smart little mouth you got there...Look, let me speak to your sister, or, next time I see your mother, I'll tell her what you said...okay, but tell Ruth I called. And if you don't, I'm going to tell your mom you're a little freak.
(Leah hangs up, dials again and mutters—)
What a jerk. Hello, Mrs. Plitt. Did Brittany come home yet? Well, what time is band practice over? Okay, please tell her to call me the second she gets home. Thanks.
(She hangs up and dials again.)
Caleb? Oh, sorry, Mrs. Plitt. I dialed your number again, by accident. I meant to call Ruth. And then when I heard it was you, I was going to hang up, but I remembered you have Caller ID so, that's why I didn't. You know, I didn't want you seeing it was my number and thinking I was trying to stalk you or something. I'm trying to get my Dad to get caller ID, but he says it's a waste of money. But you know if someone's trying to prank call you or something, then I think it would be valuable to see who it is.

(cont. next page)

Leah
(The Talk-A-Holic cont.)

'Cause, who wants somebody just calling you to waste your time? I hate people who call and all they do is blab, blab, blab, you know?

I mean, I'm sure you agree that time is too valuable to spend all day on the phone. Well, I know you're busy, so I'll let you go. Sorry I called you again by mistake. Please tell Brittany I called. And if I'm not home, you know, if I go out to get some pizza or something, tell her to call my cell phone. But, wait! I forgot to charge it last night. Ashley called me when my Mom and I were at Wal-Mart, and she was having an emergency. You know Sam, the guy that took Brittany to the spring dance? Well, he asked Ashley out so she was freakin', and she called me, and so I'm at Wal-Mart, and I just sat down by the garden hoses, and we liked talked forever, so the batteries may be dead. So, if I don't return her call, then tell her to beep me. And then I'll use the pay phone at the Pizza Hut to call her back. And if I go to McDonalds, I'll use their pay phone in the parking lot. No, wait. I don't feel like McDonalds, maybe I'll go to Wendy's. Oh, but they don't have a pay phone. Okay, whatever, I'll go to Pizza Hut. So, tell Brittany to first call here and then...Okay, I'm sorry! Just have Brittany call...oh, that's my call waiting, bye.

(Leah hits the call-waiting button.)

Hey! Caleb, what do you want? No, I am going to tell your mom if you don't tell Ruth I called...Don't get all upset. Just tell her I called and I won't tell your mom. Where is Ruth anyway? Sam? Sam Rogers? Where did she go with Sam? Okay, forget it. Don't tell Ruth I called. No, wait! Tell her I called,

(cont. next page)

Leah
(The Talk-A-Holic cont.)

but I don't want her to call me back. And in fact, I don't want her to ever call me again. Not at home. Or on my cell. And tell her my Dad is going to get Caller ID so she better not try to prank call me either! Got that? No, I won't tell your mom. But tell Ruth what I said.

(Leah hangs up and dials again and mutters.)

OH! I HATE ANSWERING MACHINES. Ashley, I just found out that Ruth is, right now, on a date with Sam. Even though he asked you out last night and he asked me out at lunch. Can you believe that? Call me when you get this. If I'm not at home, call my cell. No, wait! Beep me. I'm going to McDonalds, so I'll use the pay phone in the parking lot to call you back.

(She hangs up and dials again.)

Mrs. Plitt, it's me again. I just called to tell you I'm not going to Pizza Hut. I am now going to McDonalds. 'Cause Sam, you know, the guy that Brittany went… Oh, yeah, right. Anyway, he is at Pizza Hut with Ruth Martin. Even though he asked me out today at lunch. Of course I said no because he took Brittany to the…right. But I just wanted to tell you that I would not go out with someone who went out with my best friend. So, please tell Brittany to beep me and I'll use the pay phone…okay, you don't have to get all mad!

(Leah hangs up and mutters.)

Some people act like you are wasting their time.

(She grabs her cell phone and her beeper.)

Oh, shoot! My batteries are dead on my beeper!

(She dials again.)

Mrs. Plitt? It's me again. My batteries on my beeper are…Mrs. Plitt? Mrs. Plitt…I think she hung up on me.

Lee
(The Election Speech)

(Lee walks up to the podium.)

Student body, faculty, my name is Lee Davison. And I want to be your Student Council President. I know most of you have never heard of me. Well, that's because, unlike you, I haven't wasted my last three years trying to be popular. And I see no reason to start now. Vote for me or not, I don't care. But if you do, and I win, you won't be sorry.

Unlike my opponents, who just gave those lame speeches, I will never lie to you. I will never tell you I'll do something if I can't do it. So, what will I do? Nothing. As Student Council President, I will do absolutely nothing. But I will do it brilliantly. And because I will do nothing, you, as the students of the school, will have to do more. You will have to get off your lazy butts and take control of your school year.

You want a prom? Then you'll have to throw it yourself. I mean, come on, the proms the Student Council organizes are lame anyway. You want better food in the cafeteria? Then you'll have to stop eating the garbage they are serving until the cafeteria goes broke and they decide to cook food we can actually eat! You see, if I do nothing, you'll be forced to do more. And because there are only one of me, and five hundred of you, more will get done. And this school will be a lot better if we all pitch in. So, a vote for me, Lee Davison, is a vote for you. Thank you.

Meredith
(Kissing Up)

(Meredith is standing in front of her English class.)

Before I give my report, I want to say that I am not kissing up. Okay. Here goes.
(Meredith pulls out her paper and starts to read.)
"My hero," by Meredith. My hero is my English teacher Mrs. Xander. Mrs. Xander is the best teacher I've ever had. In fact, I know for a fact she is the best teacher in the entire school. Last week, I made a web page for her. And I wrote what a great teacher Mrs. Xander is. And people from around the world have emailed me back. And they say that they wish they had Mrs. Xander for their teacher. So I think Mrs. Xander is probably the best English teacher in the world. I know a lot of students in this class are puzzled why I picked Mrs. Xander for my report. Why didn't I pick someone else like Mother Teresa, Princess Diana, or Oprah. Well, let me tell you. Those women are very important, but not as important as Mrs. Xander.

Everyday, Mrs. Xander comes into class and tries to teach us. And it's not her fault we never learn anything. It's not her fault that English is boring. It's not her fault that she talks so soft that it puts us to sleep. If I listened to her, I bet I would have gotten an A last semester instead of a D plus. Well Mrs. Xander, I hope this report makes you understand how much you mean to me. I hope it also gets a good grade. Thank you.
(Meredith goes to sit down. Then she jumps back up.)
Oh, I almost forgot. My website address is www.mrsxanderis-ababe.com. Thank you.

Michelle
(Big Girls Can Too Get A Date!)

(Michelle comes on stage, singing.)

"I've got a boy friend. I've got a boy friend."
And do you know what the best part is?
All the skinny girls at my school like him.
(She sings.)
"But he is mine, he is mine."
Oh, did I mention ...
(She sings.)
"He is fine, he is fine."
Oh, you should of seen their faces when Frankie asked me to our Homecoming Dance. They were all standing by their lockers: Missy, Tissy and Prissy. And all of the sudden, Frankie just walked up. He was still in his band outfit.
Man! I love a guy in a uniform. And he's carrying his tuba. Uhhh! He's so strong! And right there in the hallway he says, "Michelle, I have something I want to ask you, but it's kind of hard, so, I wrote you a song."
So, in the middle of the hall, he takes out his Tuba. Missy, Tissy, and Prissy were about to die, and then he goes *(making Tuba sounds)* "Boom, boom, boom, boom, Michelle will you go to the Homecoming Dance with me? Boom, boom, boom, boom."
It was so cute!
So, of course I said "yes," and he gave me a big hug, and the tuba hit me in the head. I have five stitches.
It was so romantic!
He's coming to pick me up this weekend in his dad's VW.
I can't wait!
I just hope he leaves the Tuba at home.

Ruth
(Revenge Is Sweet)

(Ruth sneaks into her little brother's bedroom.)

Caleb? Wake up. Come on, wake up! I've got to talk to you... Shh! Mom and Dad don't know I'm in here. Look, I was in bed, got thirsty, and went downstairs, and I heard Mom and Dad in a big fight.

It was about you! Mom was saying something about you being adopted. Which I already knew, but they made me swear never to tell you. And Dad was saying something about it's time for you to go back to the orphanage. And Mom was crying. But Dad was mad. He said they had promised each other, if by the time you were thirteen, you weren't a good kid, they would send you back. And Dad says you sneaking into my room, and stealing my diary and photocopying it, and passing it around the school, proves that you are not a good kid.

Then Mom agreed to let you go, but only if Dad promised to get another baby at the orphanage while they were there. He said, okay. So first thing tomorrow, they are taking you back! I just wanted to let you know that no matter how cute the new kid is, I'll always consider you my real little brother. And that I forgive you for passing out my diary at school. Even though Jim Wolfe read it, and now knows that I'm madly in love with him. Okay, sorry to bother you. I'm sure you want to get back to sleep. I mean, this is your last night of peace before you move back into the barracks. I better get some sleep, too. Mom will need a lot of help converting this room into a nursery. Good night. Sleep tight...little brother.

Super Kelly
(Super Hero To The Rescue)

(Super Kelly comes flying on to the stage.)

Boy, it sure is a great day for flying. Not a cloud in the sky.
Wait! What's that? Oh, no! It's my evil nemesis, Dr. Armpit.
(Super Kelly lands.)
Hold it! Don't move. So, Dr. Armpit, you thought you could
escape me? Let go of that little girl before she suffocates from
your smelly underarms.
(The little girl runs to Super Kelly.)
Run and hide, sweetie, while I take care of this super villain.
Oh, and wipe your face, you have armpit sweat all over you.
(Back to Dr. Armpit)
So, you thought I wouldn't find you. Well, Dr. Armpit, you've
underestimated me for the last time. What are you doing?
No! Please! Don't take off your shoes! Aaaaaaaaaaaaaaaaaaah!
(She is forced to her knees.)
The smell! It's killing me. I've got to reach for my super
perfume to drown out the smell.
*(Super Kelly reaches into her backpack and pulls out the super
perfume. She sprays it.)*
Take that, Dr. Armpit! Take that!
(She jumps to her feet.)
Once again you've underestimated me and my powers. Now,
it's time to finish you off.
(She reaches again into her backpack.)
Here it is. Super deodorant! Guaranteed to get rid of smelly
B.O. forever.
(She sprays it.)
This is for the underarm stains you left all over the city.
(She sprays again.)

(cont. next page)

Super Kelly
(Super Hero To The Rescue cont.)

This is for smelling up the beautiful city park.
(Once again she sprays.)
And this is for refusing to put Odor Eaters in your shoes!
(Super Kelly goes wild, spraying all over.)
Well, that should take care of you. And the next time you think about visiting my city remember—I destroyed you once. I can destroy you again.
(She holds out her hand to the girl.)
Come on, little girl. Let me take you to the hospital. The sweat has burned holes in your face.
(Turns one last time to Dr. Armpit.)
So, Dr. Armpit. Let's hope we never meet again.
(Holding the little girl Super Kelly flies offstage.)

Adam
(Dude! What A Babe!)

Note: Use a surfer accent here.

(Adam talks to his friend.)

Marlon. Sorry I'm late. Oh, man. Oh, man.
But I was talking to this babe and dude.
I mean dude. She was like...dude.
See, she was walking out of Koo Ka Roo. And I'm walking in.
Because, I'm getting one of those roasted vegetable things?
And I see her, because, I'm holding the door for her
and...she...well, it was obvious she really wanted me.
So, I'm not hungry any more. Well, not for a sandwich.
So, I follow her.
Don't worry, I hid behind trees and stuff so she couldn't see.
And she's walking real fast.
Boom chick. Boom chick.
And then she stops at an ATM.
So I walk up behind her and tap her on the shoulder.
Oh, man, she starts screaming. Thought I was trying to rob her.
And I'm like, "No it's me from the Koo Ka Roo."
And she's like, "Huh. You work there?"
And I'm like, "No. I've been following you 'cause I want to ask you out."
I just did it man. Right there.
I wasn't scared or anything.
But she said 'no.'
At least I think she said 'no.'
She was running too fast to tell.
Hey, man, you want to go back to the Koo Ka Roo? I'm kind of hungry.

Copyright © 2002 by Chambers Stevens

Blake
(How Not To Talk To A Girl)

(Blake is talking to his friend, Mike.)

No, Mike, that is not how you talk to girls.
You've got to be smooth.
Girls like smooth. What were you thinking?
For example, yesterday I saw Amber.
You know, the cute chick from math?
Wow, I would love to do her equations.
So, I walk up to her and say, *(real smoothly),* "Hey, babe. What are you doing Saturday night?"
She started laughing.
I could tell I was making a really good first impression.
So I said, "Hey, I like your new braces. They really make your teeth big." I think that embarrassed her.

Girls are weird. If you give them compliments they get all freaked out. But if you don't give them compliments they get all freaked out. So, then, I was like, "And, hey, you've lost some weight. You're not fat anymore. She was like, "Thanks a lot." And then she walked away. She couldn't handle that I was treating her so nice.

Tomorrow I'm going to ask her out again. Once she has had the night to think about how great I was to her, she'll come around. What? You're already going out with her tomorrow? What she going out with a dweeb like you for? I can't believe this. I have to start rethinking my strategy.

Brady
(Nerds Rule)

(Brady is a little nerdy and small for his age. He walks up to Buck, a giant of a kid, in the lunchroom.)

Excuse me, you're Buck, right? Wait! Don't answer. I know you are. You're famous around here. Mainly for picking on people smaller than you, but hey, at least everyone knows who you are.

So, Buck, this being my first day of school and all, I was told to keep away from you. By whom? Mainly by those guys over at that table. Supposedly, it's called the 'nerd' table. And apparently, you've beat up on every one of them. Mickie, you busted his nose. Stevie, you gave double black eyes. And Pete twisted his ankle running away from you. Yeah, those guys warned me to keep away from you. That you always keep an eye out for the new kids. So, here I am! I'm a lot smaller than you, so I figure you'll want to pick on me. Maybe challenge me to a fight after school. Everyone in school will come, you know, to watch you basically smash me to a pulp. So, if that's what you want, I need to know because, I've got plans after school.

You see, I love to play on the Internet. I'm what they call a hacker. I hack into all kinds of websites. My specialty is police files. At my last school, you'll like this, it was really funny, this bully always picked on kids. And one day, he broke <u>my</u> glasses, so I hacked in to the local sheriff's files and put out an APB on him. They arrested him for breaking into a house. It seems they had his fingerprints on file for the crime.

(cont. next page)

Brady
(Nerds Rule cont.)

Of course, the bully didn't really do it. I just switched the prints with the guy who did do it. Long story short, the bully is now serving five years in a maximum-security prison for something he didn't do. But hey, they were my favorite glasses, so what do I care?

Now, Buck, you have a choice. You can fight me after school, or you can never pick on me or my new friends again. The choice is up to you.

Christian
(Pizza Prank)

(Christian runs up to the front door with a pizza. He rings the doorbell.)

(Under his breath) Hurry, hurry! You think I've got all day?

(As the door opens) Hi. Got your large hot supreme deluxe pizza without the anchovies. That will be thirteen ninety-five for the pizza. And let's see, you wanted soda, too, right?

Oh, before I forget, the manager wanted me to tell you that we were out of hamburger, so he put on some extra sausage. To tell you the truth, we weren't out of hamburger. Someone just left the fridge door open over night and the hamburger, like, went bad. When I got to work the place smelled like rotting meat. I had to go out back to barf. But, for some reason, the sausage didn't go bad. At least it looked okay. Unlike the hamburger. Man that stuff was disgusting.

So, you see why the manager didn't want to put that on your pizza. You would have upchucked on sight. Okay, here are your sodas. The total will be fifteen-fifty.

(The door slams in his face.) Works every time.

(Takes out a piece of pizza and eats it.) Ooo, there are anchovies on this.

Eddie
(Some People Are Bizarre)

Note: Every time Eddie says "bizarre," he should act bizarre.

(Eddie's hanging out in front of the 7-11.)

Hey, you! Yeah, you! Can I ask you a question? We don't know each other right? I didn't think so. Okay, so since I am a total stranger to you, maybe you can help me. And I want your honest opinion.

What kind of person do I look like to you? I want to know. Now, be honest. 'Cause every time I meet a girl, they always look at me funny. Like I'm bizarre or something. Do I come across that way to you? Bizarre? I mean, I'm a little far out, I admit that, but I'm not like weird or anything. I'm not spooky. Okay, I'm not normal. But that's good. Who wants to be normal? Not me. Well, you might. You look pretty normal. No offense. It works for you. But me, I'm definitely not normal. I'm not bizarre. But I'm not normal.

So, tell me, how do I come across to you? And pick your words carefully, 'cause I'm sensitive. Don't be trying to hurt my feelings. 'Cause then I'd have to hurt you, and you wouldn't want that. So, tell me, what kind of guy do you think I am?

Hey, mister, why are you running? Come back... man some people are bizarre.

Freddie
(Dad! I Need A Car!)

(Freddie is pacing. Then he stops and pretends he is talking to his father.)

"Dad I've been thinking. Tomorrow, when we go to get my drivers license, why don't we stop and look at cars. There's a couple of car lots close to the license place, and it wouldn't be any trouble if we..." No, he won't buy that. *(Freddie paces again.)*

"Dad, I know how excited you are about me getting my drivers license. So, just think how excited you'll be when I get me own car! "Yeah, that'll never work.

"Dad, I've saved up eleven hundred dollars and I want a car!" Hmm. That might work. "I know what you're thinking. I'm only sixteen. But the way I look at it is, if I'm old enough to drive a car, I'm old enough to own one." Yeah, this just might work.

"I mean, I don't want a Porsche or anything." Well, I do want a Porsche, but that'll never happen. "I just want a car I can drive to school and work in. And of course go on dates. And cruise in. And drive the guys around in.

So, Dad, since I saved the money, I'm going to get a car. And since you're much smarter than me about these things, I would appreciate your help in buying it. So, what do you say?"

You know, I think he just might fall for this. Now, I just have to find eleven hundred dollars. *(As he exits.)* "Mom, there comes a time in a young man's life when he needs money..."

Glenn
(Blackmail Anyone?)

(Glenn knocks on the Headmaster's door.)

Hey, Headmaster, ole buddy. I just thought I'd drop by to see how you were doing. Let me guess. Fantastic!!! I can tell by that huge grin on your face. And I bet I can guess why. Because I'm graduating! Finally, after 6 years, you are getting rid of me. No more smoke bombs in the bathrooms. No more fake vomit on the cafeteria floor. No more underwear on the school flagpole. Actually, I just flew a pair of boxers up the pole this morning. But this is the last time, I promise. Yeah, it's easy to see why you're so happy. By this time tomorrow, I'll be out of here. Adios. Good-bye. Ciao.

(Glenn starts to leave but then turns around.)

Oh, there is one more thing. I've been thinking a lot about money. My parents told me that once I got out of boarding school, I would be on my own. Thank goodness I got a full scholarship to Harvard. Doesn't it just make you mad that, no matter how mean I am, good things still come my way?

Anyway, back to money. Rereading my letter from Harvard, I noticed they pay for tuition, room, board, and books. But I was surprised to learn they don't cover spending money. Say I meet some nice girl, and I want to ask her out. I don't have any money! So, I was thinking, maybe you should give me a weekly allowance of let's say, a thousand dollars. What are you laughing at? Hear me out.

(cont. next page)

Glenn
(Blackmail Anyone? cont.)

Let's say I go to Harvard, and I start to tell everyone all the wild things I did to you. Like when I put crazy glue on your toupee. Or the time I wrote love letters to the lunch ladies and signed your name. I bet everyone up at Harvard would love my stories. And, of course, I am a journalism major. Which means I'll be writing for the newspaper.

Hey! I just got an idea. Maybe I could write about you! Yeah! You know what a great writer I am. I'm sure they'd give me a job. And just think, every week there would be a new story about how I embarrassed you. People all over campus would be buying the paper just to read my stories. Soon a publishing company would see them and want to put them in a book. And by the time I finished my freshman year in college, I would have a book on the New York Times bestseller list. Everyone all over America would be laughing at all the great tricks I played on you. Everyone in America would be laughing at you. Get that? You!!!

So, you see, Headmaster ole buddy, a thousand dollars a week isn't bad to keep your reputation intact, right?
By the way, I take checks.

Gray
(Guinness Book Success)

My dream is to be in the Guinness Book of World Records. I don't care what for. I just want to be in it. I thought about bouncing a ball against a wall or something. But the guy who has the record for that, did it for over a week. And a week is too long. I need my sleep. Then I thought about eating the most pancakes, so I had my Mom make me fifteen pancakes to practice. The record is seventy-seven. And after my eleventh pancake, I barfed everywhere. My Mom was not happy. So it can't be that. Then I'm flipping through the book, and I see this record for the fastest talker, and I can definitely talk fast. So, I've been working on it for about a month, and I'm getting really quick. I called up the Guinness people and they said you have to say as many tongue twisters as you can in sixty seconds.

You want to time me. Okay, I'll hold my hand up, and when I drop it, go. Ready. Set. Go!

(Gray talks as fast as he can.)

The big black bug bit the big black bear and made the big black bear bleed blood. Whether the weather is cold or whether the weather is hot. We will be together whatever the weather, whether you like it or not. Peter Piper, the pepper picker, picked a peck of pickled peppers. A peck of pickled peppers Peter Piper, the pepper picker, picked. If Peter Piper, the pepper picker picked a peck of pickled peppers, where's

(cont. next page)

Gray
(Guinness Book Success cont.)

the peck of pickled peppers Peter Piper picked? Theolopholis Thistle, the successful thistle sifter, in sifting a sieve full of unsifted thistles, thrust three thousand thistles, through the thick of his thumb. See that thou in sifting a sieve full of unsifted thistles thrust not three thousand thistles through the thick of thy thumb. Success to the successful thistle sifter.

(He stops talking fast.)

There! How did I do?
No way! I just broke the world record?
Yes! Yes! Yes! I am the king of the world!

Kevin
(The Poetry of Love)

(Walks to the mike with a pair of bongos.)

Welcome to the Bongo Coffee House. Tonight, and every
Tuesday night, we have poetry night. So, ladies, you are in for a
poetic treat tonight. I'm Kevin, the host. This is my last week
as Kevin. I've decided to change my name to "Jyme the Master
of Rhyme." And because I am the master, I've decided to lay
my poem on you first. Now you regulars know that I usually
write poems about my girlfriend, Judy. Or as I like to call her,
"Judy, the Master of Beauty." Well, this week Judy went on
vacation with her family, and I met a girl, Karen, and we got
hooked up and Judy found out about it. Because, it turns out,
Judy knows Karen from when they were in Brownies. And
Karen didn't know I even had a girlfriend so my poem is
called: *Poor Poor Pitiful Moi.*
(Kevin pulls out his bongos and plays along with the poem.)
Poor Poor Me
I'm as lonely as an aborigine
Reading Deuteronomy.

Poor Poor I
I can't justify
What I did to untie
My lullaby with
Judy the beautify

Judy the beauty
You are such a cutie.

(cont. next page)

Kevin
(The Poetry of Love cont.)

Please forgive me
Without you I can't see
Losing you is like suffering
From gluttony
After drinking DDT.

My life is poison without you.
My heart is all goo
Karen
Is like Serin
Who poisoned our love
You are like heaven who is always above

I made a mistake
I am such a flake
Oh how my heart aches
Poor Poor pitiful me.

(He then plays a big bongo finish.)

Wasn't that good? I worked on it over an hour. So people, do me a favor. If you see Judy, tell her I performed a poem about her. Tell her I want her back. And to please call me. But not before Wednesday. Because Karen is still in town. Thank you.

Morris
(As Good As It Gets)

(Try playing this monologue as a big nerd or a big jock.)

Excuse me, Mr. Gahan? Can I ask you a question? Yeah, it's about my math test. You gave me an A. And I was kind of wondering, why. 'Cause, you see, I got ALL the answers right. And when someone gets ALL the answers right, aren't they supposed to get an A plus?

I'm just asking 'cause, if you made a mistake, then hey, that's cool. Here's my paper. You can change it. But, if you left off the plus part just because last week I backed into your car in the parking lot, well, that doesn't seem fair.

By the way, aren't you a little too old to be driving a convertible? Come on, Mr. Gahan, you're not a teenager anymore. Get yourself a mini van or something. Old men in convertibles are kind of lame. Not that you're old or anything. Well, you're older than me. A lot older. But...anyway, back to my grade.

I think I deserve an A plus. Good work deserves good grades. That's what Miss Dean always says. Of course, you know that because I always see you over at her class flirting with her. Come on, Mr. Gahan. Isn't she a little out of your league? I mean, for an English teacher, she's a babe. And you well . . . you barely have any hair left.

So anyway, here's my test. Will you change it? *(Morris hands the paper to his teacher. He waits a beat and then gets it back.)*

B minus?

Nelson
(Popping the Question)

(Nelson walks up to Kelly.)

Excuse me. Kelly? Can I talk to you a minute?...Good... uh ... Look, I don't know if you have plans for Saturday or anything. You probably do. I mean, it's five days away, and it is Saturday night. But anyway, if you don't, I wanted to know if you might consider going out with me. To, like, a movie. And, maybe, get something to eat. So, what do you think? If you say 'no' I'll understand. I know I'm not really your type. I've never been on a date before, so I really don't have a type. But hey, if you have plans, we could do it another time. Or not. Maybe you don't even want to go out with me. Maybe you think I'm weird or something. I'm not, but maybe you think I am. I don't know, maybe you hate movies. I've never heard of anybody hating them, but maybe you do. Or maybe you don't want to go out to eat. Maybe you don't eat. Well, of course you eat. Not that you eat too much or anything. You're not fat. I hope you don't think I'm fat. I'm just big. I've got heavy bones. Runs in my family. You should see Thanksgiving at my house. All these heavy boned people sitting around eating turkey.

Why am I telling you this? Look, you don't have to answer now. You can wait, I guess 'til Saturday. In fact, you can call me before the movie starts and I'll just come over. Or we could meet at the theatre. Whatever you're comfortable with. And I'll pay and everything. I've been saving up money mowing yards. So look, if you want...What? You'll go? Great! *(He grabs her hand and starts shaking it really really hard.)* That's great! *(Letting go of her hand)* Oh, sorry. Look, I'll pick you up at, well, when ever. Just let me know. *(Grabbing her hand again)* Thank you so much! You won't be sorry. *(Letting go)* Oh, sorry again. I better go before I break your fingers. *(Exiting)* See you on Saturday.

Patrick
(Girl Crazy)

(Patrick is speaking to his mother.)

Mom, I need to ask you something. But before I do, you gotta promise never to tell anybody I asked.

Come on, really, promise!

Hold your hand up and say, "I, Mom, promise I will never use this information to embarrass my son."

Okay, good. Now...Uh...

It's kinda hard to talk about. But here goes.

How do I get a girlfriend?

Don't look at me like that. This is very hard for me.

There's this girl at school, okay, her name is Kelly Benz, and she's really hot. I mean . . .uh. . . nice.

Mom, she looks great! Wow, you should see her when she wears.... Oh, never mind!

Anyway, I like her, okay? No, I'm crazy about her. She's all I ever think about! I'm doing math, I'm thinking Kelly. I'm in history, I'm thinking Kelly. Laying in bed, I'm thinking . . . anyway . . .

Yesterday, in gym, when the coach threw the basketball to me, I screamed. It looked like Kelly.

I can't sleep. I can barely eat. Yesterday, I only had three pizzas! What should I do? I'm too scared to ask her out.

(Phone rings.)

I'll get it.

Hello?...What? *(whispers)* Mom, it's Kelly! Could you leave the room? I don't want you in my business.

Per
(When You Gotta Go, You Gotta Go!)

(Per stands in front of his teacher Mrs. Meyers.)

Mrs. Meyers? I need to go to the bathroom. No, really, this time I do. My mouth was dry before class and I drank tons of water and now...whoops...I really need to go! I'm serious!

Look, I'm not just saying this to get out of class. I really have to go! It will only take a second. I promise. It won't be like last time when Principal Duncan caught me watching cheer leading practice. This time I really really have to go. And I don't want to threaten you or anything, but if I don't go in the next couple of seconds, there is going to be a HUGE accident. A real mess. And your classroom is going to stiiiiiiiiink! And you'll have to sit here all day smelling my...accident. And then Principal Duncan will send me home to change pants. And since this is my last clean pair of pants, I'll have to do a load of laundry. And since we don't have a dryer I'll have to hang the clothes on the line. And by the time they get dry the whole day will be gone. So, Mrs. Meyers, if don't want me to miss a whole day of school while you sit in a room that smells, then LET ME GO PEE!!!!!!!!!!!! *(Running out the door)* Thank you.

Sam
(What Goes Around Comes Around)

(Sam is hanging out on a street corner. Sarah walks by.)

Sarah? Sarah! Hey, it's me...Sam! Sam Walker...
Yeah, it's me. Fat Boy Walker.
You're right. I have changed. Lost some weight. 157 pounds,
actually. Boy am I sick of carrots. Plus, I've been working out.

(Showing his muscles) Feel.
(She does.) Ow! You're pretty strong...Yeah, this is weird seeing
you again. You look good. Very good, now that your skin's
cleared up. And you hardly have any scars. No, I'm just kidding.
You're hot.

Look, I know you were kind of mean to me in last year and
everything, but I'm willing to forgive you. 'Cause that's the kind
of guy I am...
Don't apologize. We were all jerks as freshman.
Of course, you were a little meaner than everybody else. But
hey, that's in the past...
Look, I was wondering if you would go out with me sometime...Yeah, like a date...
You would? Great. How about Friday?
Wait. I can't on Friday. I've already got a date. She's great. You'd
like her. She's not at all like you. She's nice and pretty. Perfect,
actually. And smart. Oh, and so supportive. She was a real inspira-
tion for my weight loss. Hey, why am I asking you out?
Look, Sarah. I'm sorry to have wasted your time.
But really, you're not worth it. Forget I even said anything.
Oh, but hey, if you need a great Weight Watchers Meeting,
there's a really good one over on Maple Drive.

Sonny
(Home, Home on the Range)

(It's Oklahoma, in 1860. Sonny walks up to his Pa.)

Pa, can I borrow the horse? There's a new family over at the old Hampton place. And the boys over at the mill say they got a girl and she's mighty pretty. And seein' how it's a long three miles over there, I would sure appreciate you lettin' me borrow ole Red. Oh, come on! I did my chores already. I plowed the back field. I've fed all the hogs and the chickens and skinned them squirrels we shot this morning. And I've milked ole Bessie and fixed the fence where them herd of wild boar tore it down. And I'm roasting a ground hog on the fire so you'll have some good eatin' for supper. And I've made a rug from that bear we trapped last week. And I slaughtered half a dozen pigs so we'll have food this winter. And I harvested nearly three acres of corn just this morning. And Pa, if I don't get to see me a girl soon, I'm just going to spit! I promise I'll be back by sun down. Thank you, sir. Pa, I really appreciate this. I can't hardly wait. Oh, and the boys tell me the girl ain't got no Pa and that her Ma is nearly as fine as she is. Pa where you going? Pa, you said I could have the horse!

Tucker
(Where No Man Has Gone Before)

(Tucker steps out of his spaceship. He is on an uncharted planet. He speaks into his interspace communications module. It looks like a walkie-talkie. We can't hear what the mother ship is saying back to him.)

All right, I've landed. I'm getting out of the ship. *(As he touches ground)* Whoa, the terrain is soft. Spongy almost. It feels like I'm walking on a waterbed. Terry, you should feel this. It is freaky...Okay, okay, I'll do the tests. *(He pulls out his various scientific gadgets.)* The oxygen is normal. No toxic gases are detected. Hey, the temperature is a nice seventy degrees. Terry— looks like I've found paradise here. *(He starts bouncing slightly up and down. Then he starts really getting into it until, by the end, he is jumping all over the place.)*

This place is radical! It reminds me of this contraption my grandfather has back on Earth. A trampoline, I think it's called. They used it back in the twentieth century to give them the feeling of weightlessness...

All right! I'll stop messing around. *(He keeps bouncing around.)* Well, it's pretty rocky mostly. There's what looks like a small mountain range to the north, and another one to the south. The southern range looks a lot like a couple of feet sticking up out of the ground. Ugly feet. More like claws actually. Claws that are moving. Oh, no! Terry, this isn't a planet! I've landed on something's stomach.

Permission to end mission. Now!
(Jumping in to the spaceship.)
Beam me up Terry and hurry!! This thing looks hungry.

Magnificent Dramatic Monologues!

Adrianne
(Not Me)

There's a girl at my school who was raped. By her boyfriend. I didn't even know you could be raped by your boyfriend. When I heard about it, I thought it was weird. But it turns out most girls are raped by someone they know. And 'cause they know the guy, they never tell anybody. So, he gets away with it. So this girl at my school, She was like on this date. And I guess they had been going out for a while. And we started to drink. I mean she and the guy, the boyfriend, started to drink. And then he just started. And she was like, "No". But he didn't listen to her. He thought she was just—Well I don't know what he thought. But when I said "no", I mean when she said "no", he pushed her down. He was laughing. Like it was some kind of joke. And it hurt. And when he was finished, I was really mad at him. Really mad. And I got out of the car. And walked home. And I'm thinking, how did this happen to me. He was my boyfriend. And when I got home, my mom asked me what was wrong. And I thought about all those girls who never told anyone. They had a secret. And they never told. And the secret was inside of them eating away at them. But they were too scared to let it out. And I thought of all those girls and I knew I couldn't let it happen to me. So I told my mother. I was crying. And we went somewhere, this clinic, and the people were very nice. And the police came. And I had to tell them. It was scary. But they were very...understanding. And then they arrested him. Just like that. He's in jail. And I try not to feel bad for him. But I do. Because his life is ruined. Why did he do that to me? I just want to ask him. Why?

Christie
(Daddy Wanted A Boy But He Got Me Instead)

(Christie walks to center stage bouncing her basketball.)

I used to hate my Dad. He never wanted a girl. He actually told me that. He did! He used to say, "I always wanted a boy I could hang out with, but instead, I got you." So we didn't talk much.
He never came to my school plays.
He never came to my dance recitals.
He only gave me an allowance 'cause Mom made him.
Then, in junior high, I started playing basketball. I told him I was trying out for the team and he said, "Really?" That's all he said, but I could tell he was a little interested. So, everyday after school, I went to practice. And guess what? It turns out I'm like really a good basketball player. I am!

So, a couple of days before the big game, our coach comes in and tells us that the boys' gym has water damage. And we have to give our gym to the boys' team. I said, "When do <u>we</u> practice?" And the coach said, "We don't. We are going to cancel girls' basketball this year until they get the boys' gym fixed."

So, I go home. And my Dad is sitting at the kitchen table reading the newspaper like he does everyday. And I walk in and he says, "Why are you home early? They kick you off the team?" And I tell him what happened and he gets furious and starts screaming, "Nobody is going to treat a daughter of mine like that!" And he calls all the other dads of the girls on my team. And they all go down to the school. And I don't know what happened, but I heard the Principal was pretty scared. Anyway, that was three years ago. And I've played every year. This year I made All-Stars. Oh, and my Dad? He's seen me play every game.

Jennie
(Friends Forever? Apparently Not)

My best friend, Evie, is obsessed with her boyfriend. We used to hang out all the time. But now, she's always with him.

His name is D.J. Everyone at school says it stands for Dumb Jock. And I think it's true. He's been held back twice. But Evie thinks he's hot. And 'cause he's a jock, Evie is now in to sports and school spirit and stuff. She goes to all the games and screams her head off. "Go, D.J., Go!" It makes me sick.

I called her yesterday, and her mom said she couldn't come to the phone 'cause she lost her voice. This is not good 'cause Evie is a singer. We both are.

This summer, we planned on starting a band. It's going to be so cool. So, I told her mother to have Evie call me when she can. Then her mother tells me, she and Evie got into a big fight. Long story short, Evie doesn't want to start a band. She wants to stay around here so she can hang out with D.J. It seems D.J. asked the coach, and he said Evie could help out with the football team. Doing what, I don't know. I guess water girl or something. I wanted to vomit. So, I ran over to Evie's house.

We got into a huge fight. We were screaming and everything! Well, I was, Evie can barely talk. She said I wouldn't understand 'cause I've never been in love. And she's right. I haven't. But so what? I still wouldn't let some guy get in the way of my life.

J'me
(Family Feud)

(J'me speaks to the audience.)

My mother is driving me crazy! She hates my boyfriend. And she's all over my case about it. I told her Romeo is a nice guy. But she goes on and on about his parents and how they did something to her and my Dad, like, a million years ago. I'm like, "What? What did they do that was so horrible?" And she goes on and on about how the Montgomery's are bad people. But she never tells me what they did.

Romeo's parents are just as bad. They hate my parents, too. Romeo thinks his dad and my Mom used to go out. And then my Dad stole her away and now they hate each other. Maybe, but I doubt it, 'cause Romeo's dad is buck ugly. I hope Romeo doesn't look like that when he gets older.

Anyway, I was talking to our priest, Father John, about our parents the other day. He said as long as he's been in town, our families have hated each other. What a major bummer. He's prayed for them a long time, but nothing seems to work. I told him, when Romeo and I get married, they are going to have to get over it, or never come to our house.

Can you imagine Christmas with our families? My Dad would be carving the turkey. Then Romeo's dad would make some smart remark. Then my Dad would start carving up his dad. What a nightmare. Romeo and I should just run off and get married. That would show them. Yeah, that's what we should do.

Kara
(My Mom Died)

(Kara talks to her father.)

Daddy, can I talk to you a second? It's about tomorrow. I've been thinking. Sometime during the funeral, I should say something...about Mom. You know, how much I loved her, and . . . everything. How she took me to all those ballet classes, and how she'd never let me quit.

Maybe I could say that I owe my dancing career to her. Then, I thought I'd talk about the cancer. You know, how she never gave up even when she lost her hair. And how I'll miss her. How we both will. But, Dad, I've got to tell you, I'm glad she's not in pain anymore. She's finally at peace.

Hey, Dad, don't cry. I need you to be strong. Mom would have wanted it that way. Mom was so strong. I used to hate her for that. Maybe I could say something about how she lost her hair from the chemo. And how it made her even sicker. But she wouldn't quit. I don't think she wanted me to see her quit. I'm gonna miss her. We both will. But seeing her in all that pain. It wasn't right.

I'd like to talk about that tomorrow. How proud of her I am. It'll be hard standing up in front of all those people and everything. But I want to do it. For her. She would have wanted it that way.

Katie
(Straight-A Blues)

(Katie confesses to Matt.)

See this?
(She holds up her report card.)
It's my report card. Straight A's. This is my 48th report card with Straight A's. I have never even got an A minus!

So, I know what you're thinking. That girl is smart. Well, I'm not. I'm just average. But I work my behind off to get these A's. And for 48 report cards, I've done it. And my parents are proud. Boy are they proud. Every time they see me, they put an arm around me and say, "Katie, we are so proud of you!" And then, I go to my room and study, because if I don't, I'll make, heaven forbid, an A minus. And then, my class rank would go down. And then, I might not be Valedictorian. And ever since I was born, that's all my parents have wanted me to be. Valedictorian. So, I study. I don't have time for any thing else.

No TV. No sports. No friends.

Oh, sure, I know a couple of people from the math team. But we never talk outside of school, 'cause they're too busy studying, too.

So, when Mr. King asked me if I wanted to do a little tutoring, I jumped at it. Finally! A chance to do something besides studying! And when I found out it was you I would be tutoring, I couldn't believe it!

(cont. next page)

Katie
(Straight-A Blues cont.)

I've had a crush on you since first grade, when Mrs. Kline made you stand up in front of the class to sing your ABC's. Remember? And you mixed up and put 'n' before the 'm'. Everyone laughed. Except you, of course. You looked sad, and I remember being sad, too. Not because I felt sorry for you. But because I used to put the 'n' before the 'm', and my parents made me sing that stupid song a hundred times 'til I got it right. So, we were just the same. And I wanted to tell you that. But I didn't. 'Cause I guess I thought you would be embarrassed or something. But now, all these years later, I'm the one who's embarrassed that I never said anything.

Matt, I like you. And I know that maybe I'm not your type or whatever. But I like you. Not because you're popular. Or because everyone thinks you're cool. No, I like you because under all that, I see the little boy who puts his 'n' before his 'm'. And I know that little boy is, believe it or not, a lot like me.

Molly
(Crime Doesn't Pay)

(Molly is in jail.)

The first time I ever stole something I was eight. This brat up the street, Mary Margaret Warburton, had a Malibu Barbie beach house. Which I did, too! But she had the car. It was pink. And one day, I was at her house and I saw the Barbie car just sitting under a beach towel by their pool. So, I just threw my towel over it. And took it. It was so easy. Couple of days later, my mom finds the Barbie car and she goes ballistic. Throws me in the car,—the real one not the Barbie one—and drives me up to Mary's house. Makes me go up to the house—by myself—and apologize for being "a thief" as my Mom called me.

Mary Margaret's mom opens the door. And I'm scared out of my mind. So I say, "Hey, Mrs. Warburton. I found this in your front yard." Just like that, I lied. Eight years old. And she looks at me, pats me on the head and says, "Aren't you sweet?" She totally bought it. And my Mom never knew. I had gotten away with it.

From then on, I started stealing all the time: change from my Mom's purse; candy from the store; cash from teachers at school. The more I stole, the more I wanted to steal. It was like some sort of a challenge.

Then it happened. I decided to steal something really big.

(cont. next page)

Molly
(Crime Doesn't Pay cont.)

I had already stolen a bunch of bikes. There's this guy down-town who buys them from me. Anyway, it was a couple of days before I got my license, and I'm riding this ten-speed I swiped from out front of the Kwik Sack. And I'm heading downtown, when I see this car.

It looks exactly like the Malibu Barbie car. And no one is inside it, and the engine is running. Some woman was picking up her dry cleaning, and she had just left it running. So, I don't know, I just took it. And I'm driving along and it's cool, when all of a sudden, I feel something wet on my face, something licking me. It scared me to death. So I swerve to get this thing away from me and I run into a telephone pole. It turns out the lady had left the car running cause her dog was in there. And she was trying to keep the little mutt cool. So that's how I ended up in here. I hope to get out in a couple of months. And when I do, I'm giving up stealing for good.

Sawyer
(Good Dogs Go To Heaven)

(Sawyer is talking to her dog.)

Newman, are you feeling any better? Oh, look! Your nose is so cold. Here, let me wrap you up. Is that better? I know you've been feeling bad. Mom says you are in a lot of pain. And that you will never get better.

At first, I was mad. I told her you would get better, but you haven't. You've only gotten worse. So, Dad says we have to take you to the vet, and put you to sleep...forever. He says it won't hurt, and that even better, you won't be sick any longer.

I asked him if you will go to heaven. He says he doesn't know if dogs go to heaven. But I know they do. So when I die, you better find me up in heaven. I'll look just like this, but I'll be a lot more wrinkled. I love you, Newman.

Simone
(Not Ready For More)

(Simone is sitting in the car with her date, Danny.)

Wait! Wait! I'm sorry, Danny, but I don't feel right about this. We barely know each other. I mean, I like you, it's just...you know, I don't know you that well.

To some girls, that might not be a big deal. But...uh...to me, it is. Look, let's just get to know each other, okay? You know, we can have fun without...being stupid. I mean, I like kissing you it's just...I'm not ready for, you know.

(Danny rolls his eyes.)

Why did you do that? Roll your eyes like that?

(Simone starts to get angry.)

What? You don't want to talk now? What? You're going to be a big baby? You know, I think you're not that interested in getting to know me at all. You just asked me out because you think I'm easy or something. And I'm glad I found that out now before I really started to fall for you.

(Simone grabs her stuff and starts to get out of the car.)

Bye, Danny! Oh, and do me a favor. Lose my number.

Zahava
(Let Freedom Ring)

Note: Try this monologue with a foreign accent. It works better if Zahava has a hard time speaking English.

We had to move.
It was too dangerous in our country.
One day, my sister and I, we were out playing with the marbles.
I was winning as usual.
When a man comes, came, over the fence, and grabbed my sister.
My Dad has lots of enemies.
He says, *(have trouble with this word)*... democracy... makes lots of enemies.
Why does freedom make people angry?

My sister bit him.
The man—she bit him on the hand.
And he yelled out.
So our dog, Yasha, came running and chased him away.

The next day we moved.

Sometimes I worry he still sees me. And he is waiting to take me away. That is why I wear this St. Michael *(have trouble with this word)*...medallion.
My sister has one, too.

My Dad, he says, "Freedom is important."
And that someday our country will be free.
With St. Michael on our side, I know he's right.

BJ
(Afraid To Go Home)

Sometimes my Daddy and I really get into it. It's worse since Mama died. A lot worse. When I was little, he didn't do much. Like a job or nothin'. He collected disability for an accident he had on the oil rig. But I couldn't never see nothing wrong with him. Expect maybe he drank too much.

Mama worked at the processin' plant canning vegetables and stuff. We needed the money, but I think she just liked getting away from him. Most of the time when she got home, he was gone. To Sammy's, or that bar over near the racetrack. If we were lucky, he'd come home when I was in school. That way, we didn't see him much. Sometimes he'd come home earlier. Then he and Mama would get into it. Once I stepped in the middle of it. 'Cause I was afraid he was gonna hit her. And he nearly broke my arm.

To his credit, he got clean when Mama got sick. He was there for the hospitals and doctors and such. But as soon as she was in the ground, he was back at the drink. Only now he drank in the house. And if I thought he was mean before, last night, he told me to run up to the Kwik Shoppe for a bottle. When I told him I ain't gonna do it, he started swingin'. One near landed on my jaw. I locked myself inside the bathroom, but he just stomped that door down. Thank goodness he can't run as fast as me. So, you see why I'm not too excited about going home tonight. Do you think I could sleep here?

Karl
(Tattoo Troubles)

(Karl addresses audience.)

The second I'm eighteen—I'm getting a tattoo. They're so cool. My Mom is going to freak! One time, I got this cool tribal symbol on my arm. It was fake, and it only lasted a couple of days. But when she saw it, she thought it was real. She went and called Dr. Cleasby to see about getting it removed. It was wild! Till I told her it wasn't real. Then she got real angry and junk. It was bad, man. She's so judgmental. She said people with tattoos are criminals. I tried to tell her kings in ancient Egypt got tattoos, but she wouldn't listen. She never listens.

My Dad's even worse. I begged him to let me pierce my tongue. But no! He just freaks out! But, hey, at least he's not ignoring me. They're always ignoring me. Till I do something they think is wrong. That's what I like about tattoos. Tattoos get you noticed. Gotta go. My friend Z is shaving my head.

Levi
(Confession Of A Drug Addict)

(Levi addresses the audience.)

I'm a drug addict. I started with beer. Then whiskey. Then pot. Marijuana. And then, I moved up to coke. And before I got clean, I was shooting heroin.

I'm a drug addict. And I'm not here to tell you that drugs ruined my life. They didn't. I ruined my life. Me. Drugs are just the way I choose to do it.

And it wasn't about peer pressure. 'Cause no one forced me to take drugs. I did them 'cause they made me feel good. So good that I had to keep doing them. Until one day, I'm lying around, and I feel this water running into my mouth. Tons of it. And I think I'm tripping or something. But I'm not. I'm in the gutter and filthy water from the street is running into my mouth. I sit up before I drown. Drugs are not worth it. They don't make you feel <u>that</u> good.

So, I got clean. It was hell getting all that junk out of my system. But I've been clean for over a year. Now, I'm not just some kid telling you never to do drugs. That it's a waste of your life. You probably wouldn't listen to me anyway.

But I'll tell you this. You do them, you <u>will</u> get hooked. You don't think you will, but you <u>will</u>. And when you are hooked, one of two things will happen. Either you'll wake up in the sewer, like I did; or you won't wake up at all.

(cont. next page)

Levi
(Confession Of A Drug Addict cont.)

And everybody in this room will be standing around at your funeral thinking, "What a waste."

So, do what ever you want. I don't care. It's hard enough looking after my own self. But if you do decide to get messed up with drugs, don't expect me to come to your funeral.

Dramatic Monologues for Teen Boys

"Shy" Nate
(Tired of the Gang)

Everybody in my neighborhood is in a gang. I've been in the Thugs *(Does a gang symbol with his hands)* since I was eleven. I was the youngest to ever get in. They jumped me. That's what they do when you decide to join. And they hit you hard to see if you can take it. And I went crazy, swinging. Man, I was, like, *crazy.* I hit Stein in the face. The guy's a wall. His name is Frankie, but they call him Stein because he's as big as that monster guy, Frankenstein. And I'm, like, swinging, and I hit him in the face. He starts laughing. Then all the guys start laughing. Then Stein says, "Well, he ain't Shy.", and that's how I got my name.

Shy. Girls love it. They think it's cute. It gets me what I want. Now I'm the oldest of the Thugs. Well, the oldest that ain't in jail. Or dead. And everybody's lookin' at me like I'm the leader or something. But I'm thinkin' of getting out. Jail ain't for me. Someday, somebody's going to be in my face and I'm goin' to have a problem with that, and then it's goin' to be over. And one of us will end up in jail or splattered on the street. The younger guys think the police never catch nobody. But they do. All the time. They even catch you for stuff you didn't do. The way I see it, sooner or later I'm going to end up in trouble with somebody. That is, if I don't get out.

Orion
(Mad At Amy)

(The more Orion talks, the madder he gets.)

I got a call from her mother that Amy had killed herself.
She was crying so hard at first I didn't know who it was.
Amy's mom is great.
Every time I was over there, she was, like, so cool.
And on the phone she said that Amy had taken some pills that Amy's dad took for his heart.
The whole bottle.
They tried to pump her stomach and stuff but...I guess it was too late.
It was weird, Amy's mom calling me.
I didn't know what to say.
I said I was sorry and stuff. But I felt fake, 'cause when she told me, I didn't feel sad at all.
I mean, Amy was, like, one of my best friends.
But man, her Mom telling me this stuff made me furious.
I mean how could she do this?
All these people, her parents, her friends, they all care about her. And she takes this bottle of heart medicine?
Then Amy's mom says there was a note.
Amy wrote that she had too much pressure in her life. Too hard.
Too hard?
She made, like, perfect grades. And she was popular.
And next year, everybody thought she had a chance at winning something in the student council.
Yeah, Amy, that's really hard. I feel real sorry for you.
Man, I wish I would have known what she was thinking.
Maybe I could have done something.

Paul
(The Catch)

I'm at the forty-yard line. I had broke away early, and I'm really hauling it. 'Cause we only got ten seconds left in the game, and we're behind by one. So, I'm at the forty, the thirty, the twenty. Our quarterback has never thrown the ball this far in his life, when I see it coming to me. Almost floating. Two guys from their team are almost on me. And I jump, and it touches my fingertips and lands right in my hands. And the next thing I know I've crossed over the line. And they go wild, the crowd. My team is all over me, lifting me up and carrying me around. It was, like, a blur. For days, I was just happy. Smiling like I had been to the dentist, and he gave me too much laughing gas.

One night, I wake myself up laughing. See, I had not only won the game, but the playoffs. People were talking to me that have never talked to me before. "We knew you could do it. We always believed in you." The Principal keeps calling me "The Boy We All Love." Which is strange, but he's cool.

And then, the next game, the championship. I come running on the field, and I see the Pep squad had made all these banners with my name on them. And the cheerleaders are chanting my name. So we play, and it's a good game. We score one. Then they score. And it goes on and on like this for the whole game. And then at the end we are behind by one and again there are ten seconds left in the game. And I brake away early. And I'm at the forty, the thirty, the twenty, and the quarterback throws the ball. And it's coming at me just like last time. Deja vu. And it touches my fingertips.

(cont. next page)

Paul
(The Catch cont.)

Just like last time. But this time it bounces off. And I hear the crowd, they take one huge massive gasp at the same time. Like "oh no!" And these two guys from the other team are on me and I jump. High, too. And I catch that ball and they knock me down. But over the line. And when the pile up is over I'm still holding the ball. So we win. And everybody's clapping and going wild.

Except for me. Why? 'Cause they gasped. The crowd, they said they believed in me. But they didn't. They gasped. Like I was going to let them down. Like I was going to let the team down. But when I jumped, it wasn't for them <u>or</u> the team. It was for me. I wasn't going to let myself down.

That's what I learned that day. And that's why I play like I do. People's praises come and go. But the only person you have to really worry about is the guy who is looking back at you in the mirror.

Reid
(The Shooting)

Billy Brook was across the table. I never eat with Billy, but that day, I saw him just sitting there by himself, so I sat down. You know, he doesn't have that many friends. So, he's really surprised. We started talking, about the food mainly. You know how bad school food is. And then I see Billy's face go white. He has a hamburger in his mouth and he just stops chewing and looks at me, behind me, with this wild look in his eyes. And then, I heard them.

The gunshots. I flipped around, and they were coming in to the lunchroom. I had seen one of them before, in study hall. And they had on the long black coats, like the people on TV talked about. And they are holding these huge guns. Bullets are flying everywhere. Billy flips the table over. And in a flash he's behind it. Looking at Billy, so skinny and everything you wouldn't think of him being so quick to turn over this table. But he did.

It was then I saw this teacher. I don't know his name. But I think he teaches science or math, something like that. And he's heading for one of the kids with guns. He gets really close. But they shoot him.

Girls start screaming. Everyone's running out of the cafeteria. And bullets. I hear all these bullets. Then I feel this hand. It's Billy's and he pulls me behind the table. And it was then, that the guys with the black coats start running around shooting everybody in sight. And I'm sure they would have shot me, too.

(cont. next page)

Reid
(The Day I Almost Died cont.)

But Billy's got me under the table. And I'm screaming. Billy has got his hand over my mouth. They can't hear me over the bullets. And then they leave. To go somewhere else to shoot more people.

Billy turns over the table. And he drags me to the walk-in freezer. Where the lunch ladies keep all the meat and stuff. And Billy throws me in there. It's cold. And he grabs some more kids. One girl's face is bleeding. A bullet had grazed her. And we, ten or eleven people, are all crammed in this freezer. And then Billy grabs some tablecloths to wrap us in. Then he starts kicking the wall. At the time, I don't know why. Later, though, I figure out it was the thermostat. He was breaking it so we wouldn't freeze. Then he slams the door.

Everybody is just standing there. No one is saying anything. But Billy is grabbing boxes of frozen hamburgers and he's blocking the door. And that's where we stayed for the next four hours. When the SWAT team came, they led us out. And I got my first good look at the cafeteria.

It was crazy. All these bodies, just, lying there. And I realized that I would be lying there, too, if it weren't for Billy. He didn't even know me. Or anybody else he had helped. I owe it all to him. If I hadn't sat with him, I would be dead now.

Shy
(Once Burned, Twice Shy)

(Shy talks to this girl he's interested in.)

I was dating this girl, Gina. She was something.
Had a mouth on her, though.
Lots of attitude.
And she was my first girl...

You know, I'm not that big of a player. Well, when we first got
hooked up, it was kind of cool. We went places. Hung out. She
was great to kick it with. I was, like, in love. Then, she started
to get all weird. Said I was moving too fast. So I tried to back
off. But love's weird like that. It's like a dam breaking. You can't
stop the water any more than you can stop love. Anyway, she
ended it. And I haven't dated anybody else
'til you.

I'm sorry if sometimes it seems like we're going in slow
motion. But I've been burned before.
And you know...
I'm not looking to get burned again.

Skyler
(Proud)

There's this guy at school. He's...different. He laughs a lot. Giggles. You know, he's just different. A lot of the other guys pick on him. They call him "gay" and stuff. I don't know if he is. I've never see him with other guys. All of his friends are girls. But maybe.

Anyway today in the lunch room this kid was in line when a bunch of guys surround him. They start to shove him. One of the lunch ladies made them stop. They did but I heard one of the guys, Ross is his name, tell this kid he better watch out. So after school, I'm walking home and I see Ross and the guys running down the street. So I followed them. I don't know why. I just did. And we're running and running. And then I see that we're not just running but we're chasing the kid. The gay one. Well, I don't know if he's gay. But he falls down and Ross jumps on him and starts hitting him. And I don't know why but I jump in and I pulled Ross off of him. And everyone's shocked. And they're all staring at me. And I help this kid up. His name's Christian I find out later. And I start screaming. Really I do. I'm yelling, "Leave him alone! Leave him alone!!!" I guess I was pretty scary 'cause Ross and the guys back away and leave. And I help Christian home. And he's funny, really funny. And even though this horrible thing had just happened, we're laughing all the way home. It felt strange to be sad and to laugh at the same time. And tomorrow, when I go to school, I know they might call me gay, too. Not to my face probably. But they'll call me that. But I don't care. Cause what I am is what I am. And if someone has trouble with that, that's their problem. Not mine.

Dramatic Monologues for Teen Boys

Steve
(Best Friends)

(Steve and Chuck are hanging out under the stars.)

Look at that! Did you see it? That was the brightest shooting star I've ever seen. Wow! That's got to be a sign or something. You know, for good luck. Wow, that was cool. *(A beat)* You know, man, I want to say something to you. I've been thinking about it so, just shut up and listen, all right? Don't interrupt. Don't say anything 'cause this is stupid, but I want to say it.

(He takes a deep breath.)

Dude, I'm glad you are my best friend. There, I said it. And I meant it, too. Guys never tell each other junk like that. But it's true, so I said it. I hope you don't think it's weird or anything, me telling you, but it's been on my mind, and I didn't want you thinking that...well I don't know what you're thinking. But you're my best friend. And people oughta know when somebody's picked them as their best friend. So, Chuck, man, you are it. You're the best. Okay, you can talk now.

(A small beat) Don't you have anything to say? I mean, like, I'm your best friend, too? 'Cause you could tell me. I wouldn't think it was odd or anything. Okay, you don't have to say anything. It doesn't matter if I'm your best friend. Maybe your best friend is Dennis. Hey, I personally hate that guy, but if you want to associate with people like that then it's your business...What?...Oh, thank you, man, I feel the same way about you. Oh, look, there were two shooting stars at the same time. This is my lucky night.

70   **The Teens' Monologue Source for Every Occasion!**
Copyright © 2002 by Chambers Stevens

Will
(Born To Act)

I've always wanted to be an actor. Ever since I was a little guy, I'd sit in front of the T.V. acting out all the parts. My favorite was Scooby Doo. Loved Scooby Doo. I would do Shaggy and Scooby. I told my Mom I wanted to be on television when I grew up. She said, "Why wait?" And then she lifted me up and put me on top of the television set. "Look, now you're on television" And she laughed. She just sat there and laughed at me. Real supportive. But right there, at five years old, standing on that old television set, I made up my mind to be an actor.

Then, when I was six, I was watching the tube at my grandmother's house and she was watching the news or something and they were talking about trying to find the new kid for the Oscar Meyer commercials. And that tomorrow they were going to have auditions at the convention center. I talked her into taking me. All day I practiced the song. You know, "I wish I was an Oscar Meyer Weiner" And when we got to the center there were hundreds of kids waiting in line. So we waited, too. And then when it was my turn I sang my little heart out. Well, I didn't get the part, but everyone clapped for me. I was so loud that even people outside the room heard me. They went on and on about how great I sounded.

When my grandmother heard all those people bragging about me she started to take me to more auditions. After about six months, I got my first commercial. For Legos. Made over thirty-five thousand dollars on that one. We didn't tell my parents I was even auditioning. You should have seen their faces when

(cont. next page)

Will
(Born To Act cont.)

I came home with a check. That was almost as much as my Dad made. And then I told my grandmother I wanted to be in a play. And she takes me to this theatre company, and they're looking at me, like, "what are we going to do with him?"

But I told them I was born to be an actor. I had to be an actor. It was the most important thing in my life. So they started to put me in shows. And casting directors started to come see the plays. And I started to get small parts on television shows. Then I booked my first movie. And now I'm sixteen and I've done about fifty commercials and a bunch of TV shows and a couple of movies. I'm what they call a "working actor". And yet, sometimes, at night, when everyone is asleep, I go down stairs and I pretend to be someone else. Some character from a play or maybe my own imagination. And I pretend to talk to other people. And sometimes I even forget who I really am and I start to believe I'm that character. That I'm a fighter pilot or a prince or a homeless kid during the depression. I really believe it. I believe I'm that person. It's during those moments that I know I really am an actor.

The Inside Scoop

Interview with Two
Hollywood 101 Insiders

When you audition for a play, television show, or film, the first person you meet is the casting director. Two of the finest Hollywood casting directors are Susan Vash and Emily Des Hotel. They've cast numerous shows together. Some of my favorites are BOB NEWHART, THE FIGHTING FITZGERALDS, DO OVER and the pilot for SPIN CITY, for which they won the prestigious CSA award.

Before they were a team, Susan Vash cast many projects including FERRIS BUELLER (with Jennifer Aniston) and the award winning MAD ABOUT YOU (4 years including the pilot).

Emily started as a casting assistant for Jeff Greenberg. During her time with Greenberg Casting, she worked on CHEERS, WINGS, FRASIER, MY SO CALLED LIFE, and FATHER OF THE BRIDE II.

This is Susan and Emily's seventh year together. And their third as partners. Vash/Des Hotel currently cast the hit WB show RAISING DAD. (My questions are in italics.)

So what's it like casting RAISING DAD for the WB?

Susan: We really, really enjoy casting for it. It's been the best experience and we're very proud of the kids that we've cast. They're real naturals.

Now, RAISING DAD takes place in a high school where Bob Sagat works as a teacher. Bob's daughter happens to be in his class which is where a lot of the comedy comes from. So obviously, since the show takes place in high school, you have to cast a lot of kids. What do you look for in teenage actors?

Susan: The most important quality is that they are natural and don't over-act. For example, our lead actress, Kat Dennings, who plays Bob's eldest daughter, has a very real presence. She has a lot of confidence. She doesn't try to be like any other actor. She doesn't try to be like someone else you see on another show. She really has her own style.

How many kids did you see for the leads?

Susan: Oh, hundreds...

SO A KID GETS THE AUDITION FROM THEIR AGENT. AND THEY GET THE LINES IN ADVANCE AND THEN THEY COME IN TO SEE YOU. WHAT DO YOU EXPECT FROM THEM WHEN THEY WALK IN THE DOOR?

Susan: To be prepared and bring their own personality to each specific role.

WHAT DO YOU MEAN PREPARED?

Susan: To have seen the material. We don't expect them to have it memorized, just to be familiar with it. If they want to memorize the line, that's fine. Just be prepared to read with one of the casting people and know a little bit of the background, what the show is about, and the feel of the show.

WHAT DO YOU MEAN BY THE FEEL OF THE SHOW?

Emily: Like the show FAMILY MATTERS. Urkel's character was really big and over the top. RAISING DAD is more real.

Susan: We always tell them that this show is a reality-based comedy.

WHAT'S THE NUMBER ONE NOTE THAT YOU HAVE TO GIVE OVER AND OVER AGAIN TO YOUNG ACTORS?

Emily: To be more natural. Many kids come in so full of energy when they talk to us and then when they start to read they overact. They need to remember to keep it simple. Don't push too hard. When we ask them to read it like they are saying it to their best friend we often get a better and more real reading. The biggest problem is for the actor to keep her performance grounded and honest.

Susan: One thing we want actors to know is that we are not their enemy. We are here to help them and we want them to be good. When they perform well at a producer callback, we have succeeded at our job.

ONCE AN ACTOR GETS A PART, WHAT HAPPENS?

Emily: Most sitcoms start with a table reading. That's when the cast sits around a table and reads the script for the first time.
It's important at this reading that the actor duplicates his original audition. Often an actor will do great in the audition and then will come to rehearsal and get nervous.

Susan: So in other words, to avoid getting fired, bring your performance to the table. Try to be confident. Everyone is rooting for you.

AND THEN AFTER THE TABLE READING WHAT HAPPENS?

Emily: Rehearsal is everyday for about a week. The director gives you your blocking. And there are script changes daily. When the show is ready, it is filmed before a live audience.

I LOVE GOING TO SIT-COM TAPINGS. THEY ARE A LOT OF FUN. NOW, SINCE YOU WORK WITH A LOT OF ACTORS IN THE 16 TO 21-YEAR-OLD RANGE, I WANT TO ASK YOU WHAT KIND OF TRAINING DO YOU THINK YOUNG ACTORS SHOULD GET?

Susan: Classes are great. Private coaches are going to work better for some. It really is a personal choice.

Emily: Theatre experience is also very helpful for young and old actors alike. For many, the daily rehearsals, as well as performing in front of a live audience, are very beneficial. A lot of theatre actors end up being major stars whether in film or TV because they have a strong technical background.

TELL ME ABOUT A YOUNG ACTOR YOU CAST BEFORE HE/SHE WAS FAMOUS AND WHAT HAP-PENED WHEN HE/SHE FIRST WALKED IN TO AUDITION.

Susan: I cast Ben Savage when he was five or six in a pilot called WOOF. It was half animated and half live action. He was this kid with a big person-ality. He was adorable and smart and understood the role.

MRS. DES HOTEL, I'VE HEARD A RUMOR THAT YOU WERE A CHILD ACTRESS.

Emily: I was an extra on Little House on the Prairie.

HOW MANY SHOWS WERE YOU ON?

Emily: Twelve. I did it for a solid year. It was a great experience. For many kids just starting out, it is very helpful to be an extra because you can get comfortable on a set. As casting directors we don't have any issues with people being extras first. In addition, it is a great way to understand how a set works and what it is like to be in front of the camera.

Susan: If you're good, you are good. We'll hire you.

ONE LAST QUESTION, WHAT GOOD ADVICE WOULD YOU GIVE YOUNG ACTORS READING THIS BOOK?

Emily: If you really love acting, keep with it. Don't look at each audition as a failure if you don't get the part. Make every audition a mini play because you will be auditioning more than actually performing.

Susan: Right. Audition, do your best. And when you leave, leave it behind. On to the next audition.

Emily: Keep going. Keep moving forward. If there's a play in town, audition. Read from play books. Create things for yourself. Get involved in school productions.

Susan: The most important thing you have to do is want to be an actor more than anything. This means that you will get up on the stage even if you are not getting paid. You must have the passion to act and the rest will follow.

Emily: We have so many kids that come in and they want to be famous. Most actors succeed when all they can bear to do is perform, no matter what the outcome.

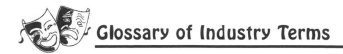

Glossary of Industry Terms

Show business has its own interesting vocabulary. Here are some words you should familiarize yourself with.

AD LIB - To make up words not already in the script. If a director tells you to ad lib, what he means is ignore the script and say something your character would say.

AGENT - A person who helps you get jobs. And then takes 10% of your earnings.

BEAT - A moment. If the script says: "A beat," then that means take a small pause before you say your next line.

BLOCKING - Stage Movement. When the director gives you blocking, he is telling you where to stand and when to move.

CENTER STAGE - Right in the middle of the stage.
(see diagram on page 81)

CROSS - When you move from one spot on the stage to another spot. This is like blocking.

CUE - Any signal that it is your turn to speak or move. If the director says "Pick up your cues," he means that when the other actor stops talking you must start more quickly.

CURTAIN CALL - At the end of the play, you come out and bow and wave to your parents.

DIALOGUE - The lines you speak from your script.

DIRECTOR - The person who is in charge of the play or film. He or she instructs the actors, set designers, and every other person/part of the play or film.

DOWNSTAGE - The front of the stage closest to the audience. The opposite of Upstage. (see diagram on page 81)

DRESS REHEARSAL - The last rehearsal before the play opens. The actors wear their costumes.

ENTRANCE - To walk on stage.

EXIT - To leave the stage.

FOCUS - Putting all your attention on one thing. If a director yells "focus," they mean "Listen up."

GESTURE - The way you move your arms and hands.

GREEN ROOM - The room where the actors hang out, waiting to go on stage.

HAND PROPS - Small items used by the actor. A purse or a baseball, for example.

HOUSE - The part of the theater where the audience sits.

IMPROVISATION - Acting without a script. Making it up as you go along.

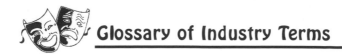

Glossary of Industry Terms

LINES - The words you speak from the script. Learning your lines means to memorize the speeches your character has in the script.

MONOLOGUE - A character's long speech.

OFF BOOK - Being able to act without your script.

OFFSTAGE - The parts of the stage the audience can't see.

OPENING - The first performance of a play.

PROJECTION - To speak loud enough for the audience to hear you. If the director says *Project*, he means speak louder.

RUN-THROUGH - A nonstop rehearsal of a play.

SIDES - Part of a script. When you audition, they give you sides to read from.

SPOTLIGHT - A bright light.

STAGE LEFT - When you are standing center stage facing the audience, stage left is to your left. (see diagram on page 81)

STAGE RIGHT - When you are standing center stage facing the audience, stage right is to your right. (see diagram on page 81)

TOP - The beginning. When the director says, *Go from the top*, she means start at the beginning.

UPSTAGE - The back of the stage. The opposite of Downstage. (see diagram below)

WINGS - The sides of a stage. If the actor stands in the wings, he/she is not seen. (see diagram below)

Backstage

Upstage Right

Upstage Center

Upstage Left

W
i
n
g

Center Stage

W
i
n
g

Downstage Center

Downstage Right

Downstage Left

Audience

x x x x x x x x x

x x x x x x x x x x x

x x x x x x x x x x x x

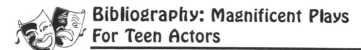

If you want to be an actor, you've got to start reading plays. I know what you're thinking, *"Oh no! I hate reading. Plays are boring."* WRONG. If you think plays are boring, it's probably because you've read the wrong plays.

Here's a list of plays you can start with. Practice reading them out loud. Remember, these plays were written to be performed *in front of an audience.* All of these plays have been performed hundreds, thousands and, in the case of Shakespeare, maybe even millions of times.

Your school library should have a copy of most of these plays. If not, they can order them for you. Most city libraries can order books from other libraries in the state. It's called an "inner library loan". When I was in high school, I used to drive the librarians crazy ordering plays.

There are four parts to this bibliography of plays for teen actors. You can't read them overnight or even in a year. Just remember that your understanding of the plays will grow as you grow as an actor. So don't rush. Enjoy!

Part I—A Place To Start

If you've never read a play before, I recommend you start with one of the following. I've grouped them by the playwright's name.

NEIL SIMON

Next to Shakespeare, Neil Simon is the most produced playwright on the planet. At every moment of every day, somewhere on earth a Neil Simon play is being performed.

Brighton Beach Memoirs - My favorite Neil Simon play. I was fortunate enough to play the role of Stanley in this one. And one night a woman laughed so hard she fell out of her chair.

The Odd Couple - A classic comedy about a pair of mismatched roommates. Also a great movie starring Jack Lemmon and Walter Matteau. There is also a female version called "The Female Odd Couple."

The Good Doctor - This is a series of short plays based on the short stories of Russian playwright Anton Chekhov. Touching and funny.

Fools - Most high school students list this as their favorite Neil Simon comedy. It's about a village where everything is backward.

GEORGE S. KAUFMAN AND MOSS HART

Kaufman and Hart are American theatre's greatest comedy writing team. Here are my two most favorite plays. If you like them, ask your librarian to find others.

Bibliography: Magnificent Plays For Teen Actors

You Can't Take It With You - One of the most produced comedies of all time. It's about a family of "kooks" who show the rest of us how to live the good life.

The Man Who Came to Dinner - When a snobby theatre critic is forced to stay with a family from the Midwest, he nearly drives them nuts with his crazy friends.

THORNTON WILDER

Our Town - This drama is one of the most produced plays by high schools. A guaranteed tear-jerker. Winner of the Pulitzer Prize.

The Matchmaker - This comedy was later turned into the Broadway smash musical Hello Dolly.

WILLIAM INGE

Inge wrote amazing plays about the Midwest. He is best known for his dramas. Did you know the best dramas usually have a little humor in them? Look for the humor when reading them. Most young actors make the mistake of playing drama "too heavy". Always look for the lighter moments. It will make the dramatic moments that much more dramatic.

Picnic - Winner of the Pulitzer Prize. Very powerful drama about two men fighting over a beautiful woman. Also a fantastic film starring William Holden, Kim Novak and Rosalind Russell.

Bus Stop - Guess where this play takes place? If you guessed a bus stop, pat yourself on the back. It's always a big hit for community theatres. Unlike most of Inge's plays, he called this one a comedy. Marilyn Monroe stars in the film.

AMERICAN CLASSICS

Here are some of the most successful American plays the theatre has ever produced. Many of them are also wonderful films. Try reading the play first and then watch the film. You will be surprised how different they are. Often characters/dialogue that work well on stage, don't work at all in the movies. And vice versa.

Arsenic and Old Lace by Joseph Kesselring: Hilarious play about two old ladies who try to poison lonely men. The film that stars Cary Grant is equally funny.

Dark of the Moon by Howard Richardson & William Berney. Just about every community theatre has produced this fantasy drama. Audiences love the romance of Barbara Allen and the witch boy John.

Diary of Anne Frank There are two plays about the young heroine Anne Frank. Frances Goodrich and Albert Hackett wrote the 1950's version. The new version was written by playwright Wendy Kesselman and starred Natalie Portman (The Phantom Menace) on Broadway.

Harvey by Mary Chase: A wonderful comedy about a man that talks to an invisible rabbit.

Member of the Wedding by Carson McCullers: A poignant story of a young girl who is forced to grow up when her older brother gets married.

The Miracle Worker by William Gibson: A play about the early years of Helen Keller. There are many great scenes for young girls.

A Raisin in the Sun by Lorraine Hansberry: One of Broadway's first hit plays about a black family. Also an excellent film starring Sidney Poitier.

Spoon River Anthology by adapted by Charles Aidman and Naomi Hirshhorn from Edgar Lee Masters. A series of monologues set in a graveyard. Did I mention that all the characters are dead?

The Prime of Miss Jean Brodie by Jay Preston Allen: About an unconventional teacher in Scotland. I know many young actresses who love this play. The film stars Maggie Smith in an Oscar winning performance.

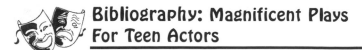

Bibliography: Magnificent Plays For Teen Actors

The Women by Clare Boothe: A hilarious comedy about a group of women who compete with each other. Check out the film starring Joan Crawford and Rosalind Russell.

AGATHA CHRISTIE
Ms. Christie is best known as a mystery novelist. But she has also written a number of plays. Most of the characters are British. So when you read aloud use a British accent. Cheerio.

The Mousetrap - This was the first play I saw when I was a kid. It is also one of the longest running plays in British history. If you like mysteries, check this one out.

Ten Little Indians - Based on Ms. Christie's novel *And Then There Were None*. The play is about ten people trapped on an isolated island. One by one they are murdered! Bet you can't guess who the murderer is.

JEROME LAWRENCE AND ROBERT E. LEE
This writing team has written a number of terrific plays. Here are my two favorites.

Inherit the Wind - A courtroom drama about the Scopes Monkey trial. If you don't know what that is, then check this one out.

The Night Thoreau Spent in Jail - Just about every college has produced this one. Very inspirational.

Part Two—Challenges

Okay, if you've read a number of the plays above, I'm willing to bet you are starting to love reading plays. And if you are reading them out loud, I know your reading skills are improving. Remember, an actor who can't read clearly will never get a job. So, if you have trouble reading, then keep at it. I promise, you will improve. Now on to more challenging plays.

AMERICAN PLAYWRIGHTS
To many actors, the most important American playwrights are Tennessee Williams, Arthur Miller and Eugene O'Neil. All three are very powerful, dramatic writers. Most of their plays are about very adult subjects. I read some of their plays in high school and I have to admit that a lot of them went over my head. It wasn't until I was older, that I knew what was going on. But there are a couple that I think you may enjoy.

TENNESSEE WILLIAMS
The Glass Menagerie - To me, this is one of the saddest plays I have ever read. Many young actors love this play. Especially the scene between Laura and the Gentleman Caller.

ARTHUR MILLER
The Crucible - Powerful drama about the witch trials in 17th century Salem. Many great roles for young girls.

Death of a Salesman - The tragic story of the last days of salesman Willie Loman. Winner of the Pulitzer Prize. Guys, check out the scene between Willie's sons Biff and Happy.

EUGENE O'NEIL
Ah Wilderness - O'Neil's only comedy. All young actors should check out the role of the awkwardly romantic Richard. It's a magnificent role.

Bibliography: Magnificent Plays For Teen Actors

BRITISH PLAYWRIGHTS

Here are my three favorite British playwrights: George Bernard Shaw, Oscar Wilde and Noel Coward. Unlike the American big three, these playwrights wrote many wonderful comedies. If you liked the films Elizabeth *and* Shakespeare In Love, *I think you will enjoy these plays.*

GEORGE BERNARD SHAW

Shaw is a wonderful writer. He is excellent at both comedy and drama. Again, when reading out loud, use an English accent.

Pygmalion - A truly great play about an English gentleman who bets he can turn a Cockney flower girl into a lady. Later made into the musical My Fair Lady.

St. Joan - Powerful play about the teenage heroine Joan of Arc. Great scenes for young actresses.

OSCAR WILDE

The Importance of Being Earnest - One of the most-performed comedies in the English language. It's about two gentleman who pretend to be named Earnest in order to woo their young ladies. Great scenes for actors and actresses.

NOEL COWARD

When I first read his works in high school, I didn't think his comedies were at all funny. Then I saw a production of Hay Fever *and laughed so hard I was crying. See, unlike a Neil Simon play where everyone walks around saying funny lines, Noel Coward gets huge laughs from people's reactions to the bizarre situations he sets up. To me, the television show* Frazier *often feels like a Noel Coward play.*

Blithe Spirit - A comedy fantasy about a man whose dead wife returns to haunt him and his new wife. Very funny.

Hay Fever - A wickedly funny play about the Bliss family. Each member of the family invites a guest to their country house for the weekend. And then precedes to treat them horribly. A play about bad manners.

MUSICALS

Musicals are often the best plays to see and the hardest to read. Because the book of a musical is only one part of the whole experience, I recommend you read these plays and listen to the cast albums at the same time. Many libraries have copies of these musicals.

Oklahoma - Music by Richard Rogers, book and lyrics by Oscar Hammerstein: The great American musical. The first musical where the dancing furthered the storyline. Check out the movie to see the wonderful choreography by Agnes de Mille.

West Side Story - Music by Leonard Bernstein, lyrics by Stephen Sondheim, book by Arthur Laurents: My favorite musical. West Side Story is the musical retelling of the Romeo and Juliet story with modern street gangs. Having appeared in this musical, I must tell you that the dancing is a blast. The film version is amazing. It won 10 Academy Awards including Best Picture.

A Chorus Line - Music by Marvin Hamlish, lyrics by Ed Kleban, book by James Kirkwood and Nicholas Dante: The ultimate backstage musical. Great songs. Winner of both the Pulitzer Prize and the Tony for Best Musical. Skip the movie. It bites.

Fiddler on the Roof - Music by Jerry Bock, lyrics by Sheldon Harnick, book by Joseph Stein: Many people consider this the greatest musical of all time. Fiddler is the very moving story of Tevye as he tries to marry off his daughters. An excellent film.

Cats - Music by Andrew Lloyd Webber. Lyrics are based on the poetry of T.S. Elliot: Andrew Lloyd Webber has written many successful musicals but none more so than Cats.

Magnificent Monologues for Teens **85**

Bibliography: Magnificent Plays For Teen Actors

Into the Woods - Music and lyrics by Stephen Sondheim, book by James Lapine: Using fairy tale characters, Lapine and Sondheim show what happens after the fabled characters live "happily ever after".

Grease - One of the longest running musicals Broadway has ever produced. My first job out of college was Kenickie in a production of Grease. This is one of those shows that is fun from beginning to end. The film starring John Travolta and Olivia Newton-John is a blast.

Runaways - Elizabeth Swados: A great musical for young actors. The songs are great. And the script which is a series of monologues about young runaways is tremendous.

Godspell - Music and lyrics by Stephen Schwartz, book by John-Michael Tebelak: A fun musical based on the Gospel of Matthew. The movie is not as good as the play.

Annie - Music by Charlie Strouse, lyrics by Martin Charnin, book by Thomas Meehan: A colorful musical based on the comic strip character Little Orphan Annie. Contains the hit songs "Tomorrow" and "It's a Hard Knock Life,"

Part Three—Thespians Love These!

Okay, if you've read all the plays in Part One and Part Two, it means you are hooked on theatre. If you read them aloud, I'm willing to bet your reading skills are fantastic! Want more? Well, okay. Here's a list of some more wonderful plays.

Amadeus - Peter Schaffer

A Thousand Clowns - Herb Gardner

Fences - August Wilson

For Colored Girls Who Have Committed Suicide/
   When the Rainbow is Enuf - Ntozake Shange

Greater Tuna - Jaston Williams, Joe Sears, Ed Howard

Master Harold...and the Boys - Athol Fugard

Mister Roberts - Thomas Heggen, Joshua Logan

On Golden Pond - Earnest Thompson

Rosencranz and Guilderstern Are Dead - Tom Stoppard

Story Theatre - Paul Sills

The Effects of Man in the Moon Marigolds - Paul Zindel

The Elephant Man - Bernard Pomerance

The Grapes of Wrath-Frank Galati
   (Based on the novel by John Steinbeck)

The Illusion - adapted by Tony Kushner from Pierre Corneille

A Man For All Seasons - Robert Bolt

Dogg's Hamlet - Tom Stoppard

Having Our Say - Emily Mann

Lend Me a Tenor - Ken Ludwig

Little Foxes - Lillian Hellman

Lost in Yonkers - Neil Simon

Miss Firecracker Contest - Beth Henley

Noises Off - Michael Frayn

Prelude to a Kiss - Craig Lucas

Sleuth - Anthony Shaffer

The Amen Corner - James Baldwin

The Colored Museum - George Woolfe

The House of Blue Leaves - John Guare

The Kentucky Cycle - Robert Schenkkan

The Sunshine Boys - Neil Simon

The Last Night Of Ballyhoo - Alfred Uhry

Part Four—The Classics

Now we come to the theatre classics. Most of the plays below, actors will first read in college. But if you want a head start, then jump in.

GREEK CLASSICS

Oedipus - Sophocles
Antigone - Sophocles
Medea - Euripides
The Birds -Aristophanes

WILLIAM SHAKESPEARE

A Midsummer Night's Dream
As You Like It
Hamlet
Romeo and Juliet

RESTORATION COMEDIES

The Rivals - Richard Sheridan
The School for Scandal - Richard Sheridan
She Stoops to Conquer - Oliver Goldsmith

MOLIERE

(Note: Moliere is the master of French Comedy.)

School for Wives - Translated by Richard Wilbur
Tartuffe - Translated by Richard Wilbur

ANTON CHEKHOV

Chekhov was a Russian playwright. Here are his three greatest plays. Stark Young, Richard Gilman and Ann Dunnigan are considered the best translators.

The Cherry Orchard
The Three Sisters
The Sea Gull

HENRIK IBSEN

The Doll's House - Translated by R. Farquharson Sharp
Hedda Gabler - Translated by R. Farquharson Sharp

BERTOLT BRECHT

Good Person of Setzuan - Translated by Ralph Manheim
The Caucasian Chalk Circle - Translated by Ralph Manheim

Index

Copyright © 2002 by Chambers Stevens